The Lord is his name

The Lord is his Name

Gordon J. Keddie

 EVANGELICAL PRESS

EVANGELICAL PRESS
16/18 High Street, Welwyn, Hertfordshire, England.

© Evangelical Press 1986

First published 1986
Reprinted 2000

Unless otherwise stated, Bible quotations are taken from the *New International Version*, Hodder & Stoughton, 1979.

British Library Cataloguing in Publication Data
Keddie, Gordon J.
    The Lord is his name: studies in the prophecy of Amos.
    — (Welwyn commentary series)
    1. Bible. O.T. Amos — Commentaries
    I. Title   II. Series
    224'.807   BS1585.3

ISBN 0-85234-224-1

Typeset by Berea Press, Glasgow
Printed in Great Britain by
Cox & Wyman Ltd, Reading, Berks.

Contents

Preface

I shall never forget my first living encounter with the prophecy of Amos. One summer day in 1970 I explored the Grange Cemetery in Edinburgh. This is a veritable 'war grave' of the armies of the Lord of hosts, for in it rests the dust of a galaxy of eminent Christians: Thomas Chalmers, William Cunningham, George Smeaton, James Buchanan, James Bannerman, 'Rabbi' Duncan, Alexander Duff, the missionary to India, Hugh Miller, the Cromarty stonemason, Robert Young of the Analytical Concordance – all are buried here within a few paces of one another. Further off stands a memorial to Thomas Guthrie, perhaps the most popular preacher in nineteenth-century Scotland, one of the two preachers (the other is David Livingstone) whose statues stand as sentinels at either end of Princes Street Gardens in Scotland's capital. There, emblazoned on the red sandstone, were the words of Amos 5:8:

> "Seek him who made the Seven Stars and Orion . . .
> Who turns the shadow of death into the morning . . .
> The Lord is his Name."

It seemed as if the great Guthrie still preached as that majestic text bore its testimony – his testimony – from his grave. That message of life was for ever written on my soul. There, surrounded by the evidence of death, was the message of life – life in a risen Saviour! The creator God, who made the Pleiades and Orion, purposes to save a people for himself. Jehovah is his name! 'He . . . did not spare his own Son, but gave him up for us all' (Romans 8:32).

The message of Amos is pre-eminently a message of new life. That message, however, comes in the context of a nation under judgement. As we shall see in these studies, Israel, like the nations of the so-called Christian West today, enjoyed an unparalleled degree of prosperity and yet was never further from the God who had given her every good thing she possessed. The contemporaneity of Amos for the practical neo-paganism of the West is indisputable. And while it affords the greatest encouragement for the true followers of the Lord Jesus Christ, it provides no refuge whatsoever for those who are 'doing their own thing' in disregard of the revealed will of God or, indeed, for those who hide their practical godlessness behind a show of nominal, outward, formal religion. God's view of our society is revealed in Amos in no uncertain terms. So also is the wrath that is to come. And, most pressing and most precious, so also is the offer of grace through the Saviour of sinners, the Son of God made flesh, the Lord Jesus Christ. May the voice of the prophet bring you to seek, with all sincerity of heart, him who turns the shadow of death into the morning . . . the Lord is his name.

Gordon J. Keddie
Coatbridge
February 1986

Introduction – Who was Amos?

Amos was a native of Tekoa, a village some ten miles south of Jerusalem in the then kingdom of Judah. He was a herdsman and a dresser of sycamore trees – in other words, he was a farmer of some means. Sycamore trees, in the Near East, are a species of fig *(Ficus sycomorous)* producing a cash crop and are not to be confused with our sycamores of Europe and North America. We know nothing of Amos apart from the prophecy itself. He prophesied in the middle of the eighth century before Christ – around 755 B.C. – and, with Hosea, Micah and Isaiah, belonged to that group of prophets who dominated this period in the history of the people of God (Fig. 2).

For almost two centuries, the kingdom of David and Solomon had been divided into two nations – Israel in the north and Judah in the south. Amos was called out of Judah to go north and declare God's will to Israel. Israel was ruled by Jeroboam II (786-746 B.C.) and was prosperous and secure, although the wealth was in the hands of a few and national life was characterized by the oppression of the poor, greed for material prosperity, debauchery and, not least, false religion. Indeed, it was with respect to worship that Israel was most offensive to God. All her other sins flowed from this polluted spring. The first Jeroboam had erected altars, with golden calves to represent God, to make it unnecessary for his people to go to Jerusalem, in the rival kingdom of Judah, to worship God in the temple – as he had commanded (1 Kings 12:28-33). Jeroboam I also created an order of non-Levitical priests. In time, elements of pagan Baal-worship crept into Israel's worship and in the disastrous reign of Ahab and Jezebel it was Baalism, including so-called 'sacred prostitution' that became the state religion (1 Kings 16:31-33; 21:25,26). A partial reformation under Jehu (2 Kings 10:28,29) was to little effect. As in our own day, when the word 'God' can mean anything from the God of the Bible to a mere psychological crutch with no reality outside the human mind, so in Israel the language of the Scriptures concealed commitments to the gods of the Canaanites. The worship of God was little more than paganism dressed up in 'God-language'.

The parallels with our own time are obvious enough, however different the circumstances. Much of what passes for Christianity in the West is a 'going-to-the-church' religion – if even that – devoid of personal commitment to the Jesus Christ of the Bible and devoid, also, of the slightest interest in, or knowledge of, the doctrinal teaching of God's Word. Ethical standards – individual and national – accurately reflect the rejection of God, his Son and his Word. As the memory of absolute standards of right and wrong goes to the grave with the oldest generation, the restraints are melting like snow in the spring sunshine and the rising tide of lawlessness and despair is as inevitable as it is heartbreaking. Prosperity – ostensibly the sign of the success of a culture and certainly something which should be seen as the blessing of God and the opportunity of doing good to others – becomes the occasion of greater oppression and hedonism and, not least, utter careless-ness about the things of God.

Amos's message speaks to all men about ultimate questions – righteousness, justice, the meaning of history, man's eternal destiny, man's relationship to a holy God, judgement and salvation. The central thread throughout the prophecy is that of *covenant relationship*. Israel was a part of the covenant nation – God's people chosen to be his own possession. They were the church of the Old Testament, given the Word of God to guide them, even the presence of God in tabernacle and temple. Yet they rejected him and, like Esau, sold their birthright for a mess of pottage. It is, therefore, to those that call themselves Christians or, if they stop short of that, still somehow think themselves right with God, that Amos's words must come with special pointedness and urgency. God, through the prophet, slices through the defences and rationalizations with which people, at one and the same time, justify their sins and clear themselves of any wrongdoing before God and men. Amos shows people who think they are going to heaven, when in fact they are going to hell, that God is neither fooled nor mocked by their self-deceptions. It is the Lord Jesus Christ who will certainly be the Judge of the living and the dead when he returns at the end of the age (2 Timothy 4:1). Yet many will say to him on that day, ' "Lord, Lord, did we not prophesy in your name, and in your name drive out demons and perform many miracles?" ' And the Lord will reply, 'I never knew you. Away from me, you evildoers!' (Matthew 7:22,23.)

God's perfect righteousness will be vindicated. Every heart will be searched. The unjust and the hypocrite will be unmasked and punished. The covenant-breaker will perish in his sins. God will turn the wicked into hell (Psalm 9:17, AV).

God's covenant is an everlasting covenant and a covenant of *grace*. He means to save a people from their sins. And in this – the gospel of saving grace – we discover the ultimate goal of Amos's prophecy: that the restored Israel of God, saved by grace through faith in the promised Messiah, would be planted, 'never again to be uprooted'. In the fulness of New Testament revelation we see that Amos preaches Christ as Saviour and Lord. And Christ himself assures us that whoever comes to him, he will in no way cast out. Believe on the Lord Jesus Christ and you shall be saved!

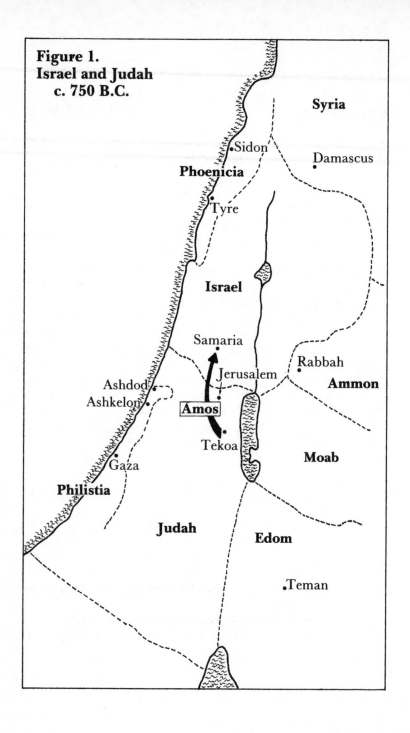

Figure 1.
Israel and Judah
c. 750 B.C.

An outline of the prophecy of Amos

  I. Introduction – the announcement of divine judgement
     to come (1:1,2).

 II. The judgement of the nations (1:3-2:16).
     A. Syria (1:3-5).
     B. Philistia (1:6-8).
     C. Phoenicia (1:9,10).
     D. Edom (1:11,12).
     E. Ammon (1:13-15).
     F. Moab (2:1-3).
     G. Judah (2:4,5).
     H. Israel (2:6-16).

III. The judgement of Israel (3:1-9:10).
     A. Five specific predictions (3:1-6:14).
         1. The special accountability of God's people
            (3:1-15).
            a. With privilege comes greater accountability
               (3:1-3).
            b. God's anger is fully justified (3:4-8).
            c. Israel's sin and the wrath to come (3:9-15).
         2. The destruction of a pleasure-seeking culture
            (4:1-13).
            a. The pleasures of excess will be taken away
               (4:1-3).
            b. Empty religiosity will fail them (4:4,5).
            c. They will ignore warnings of judgement
               (4:6-13).

   3. A call to repentance (5:1-17).
      a. The Lord laments over Israel (5:1-3).
      b. The call to repentance and life (5:4-17).
   4. First 'woe' for unrepentant Israel – the end of
      false religion (5:18-27).
      a. The Day of the Lord will bring darkness
         (5:18-20).
      b. Hypocritical worship only seals their doom
         (5:21-24).
      c. Persistent idolatry ensures final rejection
         (5:25-27).
   5. Second 'woe' for unrepentant Israel – the end of
      the pleasure-seeking class (6:1-14).
B. Five visions illustrating judgement (7:1-9:10).
   1. The plague of locusts: sent, but recalled (7:1-3).
   2. The fire bringing drought: unleashed, but
      restrained (7:4-6).
   3. The plumb-line: all to be levelled (7:7-17).
   4. The basket of summer fruit: a famine of God's
      Word (8:1-14).
   5. The destruction of the temple: the apostate
      nation rejected (9:1-10).
      a. The slaying of a sinful people (9:1-6).
      b. The sifting of the house of Israel (9:7-10).

IV. The promise of messianic revival (9:11-15).
    A. The restoration of David's tent – the New Testament
        era (9:11-12).
    B. The establishment of Christ's church (9:13-15).

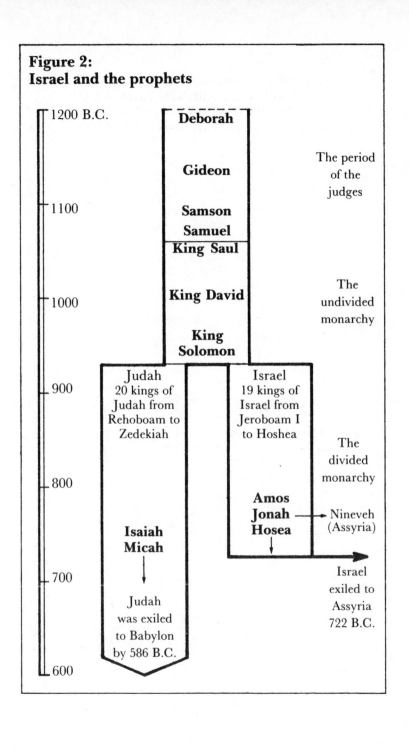

Figure 2:
Israel and the prophets

1200 B.C.

Deborah

Gideon

Samson
Samuel

King Saul

King David

King Solomon

1100

1000

900

800

700

600

The period
of the
judges

The
undivided
monarchy

The
divided
monarchy

Judah
20 kings of
Judah from
Rehoboam to
Zedekiah

Israel
19 kings of
Israel from
Jeroboam I
to Hoshea

Amos
Jonah
Hosea

Isaiah
Micah

Judah
was exiled
to Babylon
by 586 B.C.

Nineveh
(Assyria)

Israel
exiled to
Assyria
722 B.C.

1.
The whirlpool of judgement

Please read Amos 1:1–2:3; 2 Kings 14:23-29

Israel was prosperous in the reign of Jeroboam II (786-746 B.C.). In the two centuries since King Solomon's day there had never been such good times. Judah, under King Uzziah (783-742 B.C.), was also experiencing something of a golden age. They were, in the language of the prophecy, 'complacent in Zion' and 'secure on Mount Samaria' (6:1). Even so, there were still those who were poor and oppressed. And no doubt there was also a remnant of believers who grieved over the prevailing decadence and earnestly cried out to God for his reviving power to turn Israel back from her backslidings.

As in our own national experience today, Israel's relative peace abroad and prosperity at home generated the twin evils of a greedy, pleasure-seeking materialism and an easy conscience-salving formalistic religion. Those that could filled their days with the pleasures of excess. The cry for more and still more was their only answer to the frustrating transience of sensual joys. 'Bring us some drinks!' is the watchword of the social round (4:1). The 'beds inlaid with ivory' and the addiction to carousing and entertainment stand as the abiding marks of a self-centred culture that lives only for the moment and sensual satisfaction (6:4-6). On the other hand, the disquieting memory of the nation's God, with its implication of offended holiness to be appeased, and the gnawing reality of death, with the uncertain prospect of an eternal destiny in the gift of that God, were alike palliated by an easy religion consisting in the multiplication of ritual observances, never commanded by God but sufficient to ease the seared consciences of wicked people. Outward observances – not excluding the modern ritual attendances at Christmas, Easter

17

and even the odd morning service – make wonderful sops to the deeper, though suppressed, anxieties of the human conscience and to the disturbing eminence of a God whom a man knows he has disregarded in daily life and fears he must meet before too long. Empty ritual is the natural currency of man-made self-justifying religion and that is why God gives no place to it and calls for worship that is in spirit and truth (e.g. Psalm 51:16,17; Amos 4:4,5; 5:4-6; Matthew 23:23; John 4:24).

Into this society, so frighteningly reminiscent of our own, God sends the prophet from Tekoa to tell men and women the truth about themselves – to tell them of their sin in rejecting God's revealed will for their lives, of the justified anger of a holy God who cannot look upon sin, of the divine verdict on their decadent national life and their empty religion, of the impending destruction of their culture and national identity and, far transcending all of these hard words, of the way of salvation and the restoration of the Israel of God. Men who see no need to be saved hear only the words of judgement to come and, characteristically, dismiss God's messenger as a 'prophet of doom'. 'The land cannot bear all his words,' complained Amaziah, the priest of Bethel (7:10). It is no mere coincidence that the modern cartoon prophet, with his sandwich-board bearing the words, 'Prepare to meet your God,' is drawn from Amos 4:12. How better to relieve yourself of an uncomfortable truth then by turning it into a joke? Men will laugh their way to hell when they would recoil from sober opposition to the living God. What we cannot face we dismiss with ridicule. But some reject the truth with grim anger. If the message cannot be ridiculed, it can be rejected as an aberration. The very idea of the 'prophet of doom' carries with it the supposition that a true prophet would not preach 'doom'. In such a view, doom is not just undesirable but *unthinkable*. This is the same argument as that of the atheist who asserts that because there is so much misery and suffering in the world, there can therefore be no God. His 'God' is, of course, an abstract construction of his own imagination, as opposed to the real God of the Bible who has told us who he is and why he permits the world to continue on its wicked way. The argument is invalid because the atheist's 'God' is a straw man designed only for the purpose of being knocked down. Similarly the idea of the 'prophet of doom' is an excuse to avoid the real facts – both of judgement and salvation. Judgement to come may be unthinkable to sinners, ancient and modern, but it is a fact of God's Word.

The first verse of Amos's prophecy demonstrates the folly of mocking God in these matters. Amos, we are told, prophesied 'two years before the earthquake'. Over 250 years later, Zechariah remembered that first pledge of judgement upon Israel, when he said to the exiles who had returned from Babylon, 'You will flee as you fled from the earthquake in the days of Uzziah king of Judah' (Zechariah 14:5). God is not mocked! His Word is sure. His righteous vengeance is as terrible as it is absolutely just. History itself is the ever-unfolding confirmation of this solemn truth!

The Lord roars from Zion (1:2)

The prospect of God's judgement, whether upon individuals or nations, could hardly be expected to engender widespread enthusiasm. Perhaps the exception to this rule is when the 'other side' is thought to be getting its just deserts. There is no place for such vindictiveness. It is 'a dreadful thing to fall into the hands of the living God' (Hebrews 10:31). There is certainly no doubt that God's judgements are continually executed 'in all the earth' (Psalm 105:7). The destruction of Hitler's Germany or the politico-economic decline of Britain may properly be seen as divine judgements. All events in history, however small or personal, are providences; they are, in a certain sense and to a particular degree, the 'finger of God', to be assessed in the light of Scripture-revealed principles by which God deals with men (Exodus 8:19). The interpretation of events is fraught with great difficulties. The precise identification of cause and effect is surely very rarely discernible beyond the general sense that one must gain from all dramatic turns of circumstances, namely, that God has a controversy with men and repeatedly demonstrates his power and paramountcy over our lives. The old cliché is as meaningful as ever: man proposes; God disposes.

Amos, however, was sent by God to declare specific future judgements upon particular nations. History has long confirmed the accuracy of these prophecies – a fact that invests this aspect of God's dealings with the human race with great urgency when viewed in the full light of New Testament prophecy that yet awaits its fulfilment in time.

'The LORD roars from Zion.' The use of the divine name is emphatic. The name 'LORD', in capital letters, renders the covenant name of God, Yahweh, or, more familiarly, Jehovah (Exodus 3:14,15; 19:3-6). The point is that the name itself indicates God's relationship to his covenant people *and* to the whole human race. Thus Isaiah, in speaking of the future glory of God's believing people, says,

> For your Maker is your husband –
>   the LORD Almighty is his name –
> the Holy One of Israel is your Redeemer;
>   he is called the God of all the earth
>
> (Isaiah 54:5).

He is sovereign. He 'roars' by right. His law goes forth 'from Zion', that is to say, from the place where he appointed his people to worship him, the place where sacrifice for sin was to be made, the place where he revealed his glory to Israel and, indeed, to the whole race of men. He 'roars' like a lion. He is the Lion of the tribe of Judah. And, just as the roaring of a lion presages the devouring of the prey, so the Lord's roaring is the harbinger of his righteous vengeance against the wickedness of men and nations (Amos 3:8; Jeremiah 25:30-38).

'The pastures of the shepherds dry up.' The absolute sovereignty of God is further emphasized in the execution of his just judgements. Even the summit of Carmel withers – the very springs that could sustain Elijah through the drought of three and a half years in the previous century! (1 Kings 17-18.) The lesson is clear and simple: God's vengeance, which is holy and just, will be wreaked upon the whole world. As J. A. Motyer has so succinctly stated, 'The whole world is under divine observation, subservient to divine assessment and subdued without refuge before divine judgement.'[1]

---

[1] J.A. Motyer, *The Day of the Lion*, IVP, 1974, p.31.

Approaching thunder (1:3)

Each specific judgement begins with the same basic formula: 'This is what the Lord says: for three sins . . . even for four, I will not turn back my wrath . . .' (1:3,6,9,11,13; 2:1,4,6). Two points stand out in this superscription.

1.   **'This is what the Lord says.'** A series of denunciations issues forth upon the nations surrounding God's covenant people. This whirlpool of judgement draws ever closer to Israel as the approaching thunder of God's anger consumes one nation after another (Fig. 3). The nations are judged in terms of their relationship to God's people, with the sole exception of Moab, whose sin was against Edom (2:1). This is no mere coincidence. It tells us something about God's dealings with the world. His judgements are intimately connected with the redemption of his people. They are, for all their inconsistencies and failings, his people, his ambassadors, in this earth. He will correct them, yes, and with severity appropriate to their backslidings. Yet his handling of the unbelieving world is undertaken with the purpose of vindicating his cause and kingdom in their consciousness. The sins of the nations against Israel become the occasion of God's demonstration of his purpose to exalt his truth and, in so doing, actually to save people from their sins. As a matter of fact, the prophecy of Amos unfolds just such a scenario. The promise of salvation overarches the inevitability of divine judgement as the message of grace comes increasingly to the fore, rising to that glorious crescendo in the final chapter where the redemption of the people of God is promised in the most sublime language of revelation (3:2; 4:10-13; 5:4-8,24; 9:8-15).

The two divine activities – condemnation and redemption – go hand in hand but do not have equal weight in the prophet's ministry. Amos is no more a prophet of doom than Jonah will be just a few years later. Yes, there is judgement. But 'David's fallen tent' will be restored (9:11), just as, in Jonah's case, Nineveh will repent! (Jonah 3:6-10.) The primacy of grace comes out most clearly in the saving work of the Lord Jesus Christ. He did not come to condemn the world, but to save the world through his death for sinners. The point is that

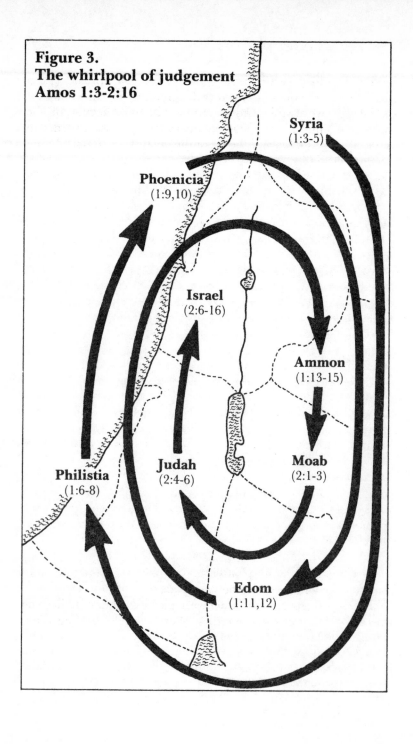

Figure 3.
The whirlpool of judgement
Amos 1:3-2:16

Syria
(1:3-5)

Phoenicia
(1:9,10)

Israel
(2:6-16)

Ammon
(1:13-15)

Philistia
(1:6-8)

Judah
(2:4-6)

Moab
(2:1-3)

Edom
(1:11,12)

'Whoever does not believe stands *condemned already*' (John 3:17,18). Christ does not need to do anything to achieve (if that is the right word) the condemnation of the unbelieving, but he must suffer humiliation, even to death on the cross, in order to save sinners. To be sure, he is coming again to judge the living and the dead, but the departure of the reprobate lost into hell is only the necessary concomitant of that central purpose of the messianic work of Christ – God in the midst of his saints, the new heaven and the new earth wherein dwells righteousness, the Lamb of God, worthy of all praise, and all that pertains to the glory yet to be revealed (Romans 8:18-21; Revelation 20:11-22:21).

2.   **'For three sins . . . even for four.'** These words are a way of saying that the cup of wickedness and injustice is filled up as far as God is concerned and he will no longer seek to turn them back. The words of Genesis 6:3 echo down the centuries: 'Then the Lord said, "My Spirit will not contend with man for ever . . ."' 'God is measuring human wickedness and there will be a reckoning and absolute justice will be served. God stays his wrath to remember mercy, but his slowness to anger is taken by wicked men as a proof of his non-existence and as a licence to go on in sin. The psalmist was troubled by the apparent prosperity of the wicked:

'When I tried to understand all this,
   it was oppressive to me
till I entered the sanctuary of God;
   then I understood their final destiny'
                                   (Psalm 73:16,17).

Men and nations are filling up the measure of sin – one at a time, day after day, year after year. If Christ will not be your Saviour, he will certainly be your Judge!

Perhaps the people of Israel were pleased, at first, to hear of the destruction of their enemies. Were they not getting their just deserts? Perhaps you feel much the same about the famines and wars that are destroying whole nations in Africa, Asia and Central America. 'No doubt, the judgements of God are abroad in the earth,' you say and console yourself that we have

the Mother of Parliaments and the EEC grain mountain
between us and anarchy and famine. Do you really not hear the
approaching thunder?

Epitaphs for the nations (1:3-2:3)

A relentless catalogue of international sin and the retribution
to follow is now unfolded. In no case will God turn back his
wrath.

1.   *Syria* (Damascus) is condemned for *atrocities* against the
people of Gilead, a part of Israel (1:3-5). 'She threshed Gilead
with sledges having iron teeth,' may refer to the dismembering
of prisoners with a device similar to a farmer's threshing sledge
of that day. For this, Syria's rulers, her capital Damascus, her
kings' pleasure resorts, the Valley of Aven and Beth-Eden, will
be destroyed and her people sent into exile in Kir, whence they
had originated (9:7).

2.   *Philistia* (Gaza) has practised *slavery*, having sold God's
people to Edom (1:6-8). These inveterate foes of Israel are to be
extinguished as a nation (Zephaniah 2:4-7). They regarded
men as no more than chattels.

3.   *Phoenicia* (Tyre) has broken her treaty with Israel and sold
her people into slavery in Edom (1:9,10). The God who deals
with men in terms of covenants takes a dim view of *covenant-
breaking*. All sin is covenant-breaking and broken covenants
between nations are but one aspect of human sin. Tyre's sin
was a sin against light, against the trust of brethren and against
a solemn promise before God and men. She too will perish
(Ezekiel 26-28).

4.   *Edom* indulged a long-standing *racial prejudice* against
God's people (1:11,12). Edom was descended from Esau and
the bitterness consumed the whole nation (Genesis 25:19-34;
Numbers 20:14-21; Obadiah 10-14). She too would be
obliterated from the roll of nations.

5.   *Ammon* was guilty of *genocidal imperialism* (1:13-15). They
were descendants of Lot (Genesis 19:30-38). In the effort to
enlarge her borders Ammon slaughtered whole populations – a
fact signalized by the murder of mothers and their unborn

children. This nation would fall and her people be exiled.

6. *Moab*, sandwiched between Ammon and Edom, was guilty of the *desecration of the dead*. The Moabites cremated the exhumed corpse of an Edomite king and ground his bones for use as mortar for building (2:1-3). They too were descendants of Lot. For their barbarism, of which this was no doubt only the tip of the iceberg, they would be destroyed.

The prophetic witness of the church

The church of the Old Testament was the nation of Israel, although in Amos's day, it was represented by the two kingdoms, Israel and Judah. The judgements upon the surrounding nations were not given to lull the church of that time into a greater – and false – sense of security. They had more and to spare of that commodity! The church would not be exempt from purging as by fire, for the *status quo* was the fundamental problem. The church had become 'the world' and must be reformed and renewed in order to fulfil her calling as God's messenger to lost humanity.

The question that confronts the New Testament church – the Israel of God of this present age (Galatians 6:16) – concerns the content of the prophetic witness of Christians today and, not least, the practical godliness with which Christians carry themselves before God and men.

Firstly, it is clear that God is concerned about vindicating his law in the affairs of all nations. God's Word claims the obedience of all men – as individuals and as nations. We, in our so-called "post-Christian" age, are too used to thinking of the Christian faith in personal, individualistic terms – as if the gospel is solely concerned with individual piety and ethics, but not with the ethics of men in the mass, in institutions and in nations. God might have spared Sodom for the sake of a few righteous men (Genesis 18:32), but the point is thereby made that Sodom was responsible to God for her sin. The nation – the state, if you like – is not neutral with respect to Scripture's moral teaching. Amos shows us that, among other things, nations are not to commit atrocities, not to persecute God's

people, not to break treaties and not even to desecrate the
bones of heathen kings! Christ has revealed himself as King of
kings and Lord of lords. He is Head over all things to the
church (Ephesians 1:22). It is Jesus Christ, not the
pragmatism of Machiavelli – the prince of politics of the West
today – who is to set the ethics of national policies. For those
nations which rebel against Christ the prophecy of Amos has
the most urgent significance. He who has ears, let him hear!

Secondly, it follows that the church has the prophetic task to
declare the mind of God as revealed in the Scriptures on social,
national and international issues. The Lord's voice is not to be
silenced – not by a 'tyranny of the experts', which disqualifies
all but graduates in political science from expressing a valid
viewpoint, not by the apathy or opposition of a vast
unbelieving majority and not by a notion of the state as a
morally 'neutral' institution, whose only obligation is to avoid
the appearance of being influenced unduly by the principles of
biblical truth. The widely held American doctrine of the
'separation of church and state' is frequently invoked as
necessary to the prevention of religious bias in public policy
and to the protection of the religious pluralism of modern
society. Whatever one's view of religious pluralism, it is
certain, from God's Word, that the witness of God's church is
to call men *and* nations to submit to Christ's lordship in terms
of the biblical principles appropriate to personal and national
life.

Thirdly, the prophetic witness of the church to the nations
cannot be separated from the gospel of salvation through faith
in Christ as the sin-bearing Substitute for sinners. Lives are to
be changed, patterns of thinking reformed, behaviour
transformed, sins confessed and repented of, and all through
receiving Jesus Christ in a faith that looks to him as the only
Saviour for time and eternity. Christ is Lord – not a social
programme or a political theory. That is the error of the 'social
gospel'. It is knowing Christ, personally, that is the heart of the
matter, from which all the rest flows, namely, the application
of the Word of Christ to every area of human life-experience.
'Believe on the Lord Jesus Christ and you shall be saved' is the
heart and soul of all Christian witness.

God has revealed himself as the one who takes no pleasure in the death of the wicked. His instruction to the prophet Ezekiel was this: 'Say to them, "As surely as I live, declares the Sovereign Lord, I take no pleasure in the death of the wicked, but rather that they turn from their ways and live. Turn! Turn from your evil ways! Why will you die, O house of Israel?"' (Ezekiel 33:11.)

Questions for study and discussion

1. What was the political, social and spiritual condition of Israel in Amos's day? Do prosperity and/or religiosity imply the favour of God? (See Psalm 73:1-20.)
2. What does Amos 1:2 say about Israel's prospects? But compare with Amos 9:8-15.
3. What is God's relationship to the nations of the world? (Psalm 100:1; 117:1.) Is God interested in them? (See Romans 1:18-20.)
4. What is the covenant nation of the Old Testament? And the New Testament? In what sense is our country a Christian nation, if at all? In what sense is the Christian 'nation' spread throughout the world? (See 1 Peter 2:11-17.)
5. Discuss the representative sins of the nations in Amos 1:3-2:3. Relate this to the policies of modern nations. How should we respond to this? Have things improved? (See 1 Thessalonians 4:13-5:23.)
6. Why is the subject of God's law and his judgements resented or ridiculed? Is the prophetic witness of the church in every age a message of doom and gloom? What was the core of the prophets' message? (Amos 9:8-15; Ezekiel 33:11-20; Isaiah 55.)

2.
The noose tightens

Please read Amos 2:4-16

If Amos had stopped preaching after that prophecy about Moab (2:1-3), he would surely have been the most popular preacher in Israel for years! It is a melancholy fact, to which experienced preachers can testify, that people love to listen to what God has to say to *other* people. 'That was a good word, Amos,' they might have said, as they left the meeting. 'Isn't it an awful world we live in? Terrible, what's going on. Still, we have a lot to be thankful for, don't we?' It is easier to hear about the world outside and all that is wrong with it than to face the 'world' that is in our hearts. Amos had so far preached about 'them' rather than 'us'. This could not but interest and excite the Israelites. One by one, these nations that had been the bane of Israel's existence for hundreds of years were declared to be under the judgement of God. What an encouraging message it must have seemed to many who heard the prophet's words!

Anyone who knew something about the art of preaching and the ways of prophets would, however, have wondered what was coming next. He might have remembered how the prophet Nathan came to David and told the king a story about a poor man who had only one ewe lamb, yet had it taken from him by a rich man who had many sheep and cattle. David was moved by this and was angry at the rich man, who he thought deserved to die, but should certainly pay fourfold compensation to the poor man. Then Nathan said to David, 'You are the man!' Then he rebuked him, in the name of the Lord, for his sin in arranging the death of Uriah the Hittite so that he could take Bathsheba, Uriah's wife, to be his own wife and cover up his earlier adultery with her (2 Samuel 12:1-13). David was led, by his own interest in Nathan's tale, to condemn himself and, as we know, he confessed his sin and repented – and, we might add, bore something of the consequences of that sin for the rest of his life. In a similar vein, but with a different result, was the Lord Jesus Christ's handling of the rich young man (Matthew 19:16-22). The fellow wanted to know what 'good thing' he had to 'do' to get eternal life. Jesus spells out some of the Ten Commandments. 'Oh,' says the lad, no doubt glad to hear what Jesus said, 'I've kept all these!' Then, just to make sure, he adds, 'What do I still lack?' 'Well,' said Jesus, 'if you want to be perfect, go, sell your possessions and give to the poor, and you will have treasure in heaven.' That, of course, hit the nail on the head, but Jesus only hit it after the young man was prepared in heart and mind to see the truth about himself in the most dramatic and inescapable manner possible.

Amos, in the same way, sets up Israel for a dramatic exposure of their desperate state. He does not stop with Moab. He fords the Jordan and climbs up the Judean hills and speaks of fire coming to consume 'the fortresses of Jerusalem'. Amos speaks about his own people, for he is a farmer from Tekoa in Judah. More ominously, he speaks of judgement upon the people of God rather than heathen nations. Now the preacher is not so popular . Who will be next for judgement? The awful truth is beginning to dawn. The words of Nathan to David echo across the years: 'You are the man . . . you are the man . . . *you* are the man!'

Covenant-breaking (2:4,5)

Judah and later the northern kingdom of Israel are dealt with in a significantly different way than were the heathen nations. 'Other nations,' said Matthew Henry, 'were reckoned with for injuries done to man,' while they are 'reckoned with for indignities done to God'. The cause of God's anger is stated in theological terms: 'They have rejected the law of the Lord and have not kept his decrees . . .' They had been given the living words of God. They had been kept by his power throughout the generations. God had delivered them from Egypt. They had been bound in an everlasting covenant, given freely and sovereignly by the God of all grace. Truth and blessing had marched side by side in their national experience, as had backsliding and chastisement. And still they threw it all back in God's face! They knew the truth, but rejected it anyway! Four aspects of this apostasy from God are now brought out.

1.   **'They have rejected the law of the Lord.'** In other words, they rejected the lordship of God for their lives. The Word of God is the only authoritative rule of faith and life given to men. This Word they rejected. The standard by which they lived ceased to be the revelation of God and now became their own imagination. They, in effect, exchanged the truth of God for a lie and worshipped created things rather than the Creator (Romans 1:25). They voted for paganism. They asserted the sovereignty and superiority of the human mind over the Word of God. They enthroned man as the measure of all things.

2.   **'They ... have not kept his decrees.'** They therefore embarked on a programme of knowing and wilful departure from God's will, by doing what they thought best in their own eyes. They modified the worship of God to suit themselves. They adjusted the 'values' governing acceptable behaviour in society. They might well, like their descendants, the Pharisees, give a tithe of their spices – 'mint, dill and cummin' – but they 'neglected the more important matters of the law – justice, mercy and faithfulness' (Matthew 23:23). They redefined sin as good to suit their own convenience.

3.   **'They have been led astray by false gods.'** They turned to idolatry. There were new allegiances now. Now, as then, when men abandon the infinite-personal God of the Bible, they turn to gods of another kind. All men without a living faith towards God in Jesus Christ, the only Redeemer of men, are indeed 'atheists' in that they live as if God has no claim upon them, as if he is not there. But all 'atheists' have their own finite-impersonal gods – the presuppositions and aspirations of evolutionary materialism, perhaps, for the thinkers, or the modern teraphim and golden calves of 'things', or power, or achievement, or, at the lowest level of all, a 'good time'.

4.   **'The gods their ancestors followed.'** Yesterday's heresy is tomorrow's orthodoxy. Tradition, in the bad sense,

prevailed over revealed truth. Canaanite religious practices were progressively adopted into the worship of the Hebrews and baptized, as it were, to the status of received doctrine. Children tend to imitate their fathers. But that will not do as an excuse. 'Do not follow the statutes of your fathers or keep their laws or defile yourselves with their idols. I am the Lord your God; follow my decrees and be careful to keep my laws' (Ezekiel 20:18,19).

For this, **'fire'** would come **'upon Judah, that will consume the fortresses of Jerusalem'.** There is surely a peculiar sadness about the falling away of those who had the blessing of God, so to speak, dished up to them on a plate. They had covenant privileges – God's way of spiritual and eternal life – but they chose the way of death. Subsequent history stands as the irrefutable proof of their folly.

Covenant-breaking is regarded by God as particularly offensive and it is answered with the severest of warnings and portents of retributive punishment to come. God's first call is, of course, for repentance and a return to faithfulness. Failure to do so is attended by fearful consequences. Indeed, covenant-breaking is dealt with more severely than straightforward paganism. The Lord Jesus Christ explains this in the parable of the faithful steward: 'That servant who knows his master's will and does not get ready or does not do what his master wants will be beaten with many blows. But the one who does not know and does things deserving punishment will be beaten with few blows. From everyone who has been given much, much will be demanded; and from the one who has been entrusted with much, much more will be asked' (Luke 12:47,48). The more light from God's Word that a man has, the more accountable he is for what he does with it. Those therefore who have the great privilege of hearing God's Word and, more particularly, of falling within the administration of the covenant – professing adults and their children (Acts 2:39) – have the responsibility to embrace the truth that they hear and discover, or else their latter state will be worse than their former condition. This is so practical a truth that it reaches to the conscience of every person every single time that person encounters the Word of God. For you who attend church and

hear the Word faithfully opened, it means that unless your
response to that Word is to receive it with joy, out of love
towards Christ and an earnest desire to be his obedient
disciple, then you may be hardening your heart and heaping
up judgement upon yourself.

The writer to the Hebrews sounds the alarm with earnest
candour: 'It is impossible for those who have once been
enlightened, who have tasted the heavenly gift, who have
shared in the Holy Spirit, who have tasted the goodness of the
word of God and the powers of the coming age, if they fall
away, to be brought back to repentance, because to their loss
they are crucifying the Son of God all over again and subjecting
him to public disgrace' (Hebrews 6:4-6).

There is a big difference, you see, between outward religion
and the inward experience of a saving change in heart and life,
through Jesus Christ becoming our personal Saviour and
Lord. Those who, in Hebrews 6:4-6, 'fall away', prove that
they were never truly converted to Christ. However good they
looked to other people, however active and apparently zealous
their behaviour, their hearts were not right with God. God
could see that they were phonies, even if hardly anyone else
could! This is illustrated in the case of the Pharisees. Jesus
called them 'hypocrites' – which word has the literal meaning
'play-actor' – and then he said to them, 'You travel over land
and sea to win a single convert, and when he becomes one, you
make him twice as much a son of hell as you are' (Matthew
23:15).

Covenant-breaking can be covered up with a lot of religion
and plenty of outward zeal, but it is all show, because in the
heart there is still hostility to God (Romans 8:7). This was the
problem with Israel and Judah.

The ethics of hypocrisy (2:6-8)

Inexorably the noose has tightened around the northern
kingdom of Israel. Amos does not repeat what he said about
Judah's rejection of God's law. It goes without saying that
Israel, with her long-standing addiction to the sin of the first

Jeroboam, the son of Nebat (the golden calves of Dan and Bethel, 1 Kings 12:25-33), had long since crossed that Rubicon of apostasy. Amos moves purposefully to recount the sins of Israel. Four examples are given.

1. *Corrupt judges oppress the innocent and the poor* (2:6). **'For silver'** judges can be bought to convict someone of a crime he did not commit. They also sell **'the needy for a pair of sandals'**, which appears to mean that a man unable to pay a small debt – the cost of the sandals – was given in slavery to his creditor. This was supposedly on the basis of God's Word in Leviticus 25:39,47, which provided for a man to work off a debt he could not repay. In Israel the rich used the slightest pretext to enslave the poor. The law designed to preserve a man's property (in that case a personal loan) was perverted, with the connivance of a corrupt judiciary, to deprive ordinary people of their most basic freedom.

2. *They enjoyed the misery of the poor* (2:7a). A modern paraphrase of this verse might be 'They wanted to rub the faces of the poor in the dirt.' The poor were to be kept in their place. It was class prejudice of the most exploitative kind. It was a species of apartheid – akin, perhaps, to the serfdom imposed upon the masses of Tsarist Russia until the middle of the nineteenth century. Oppressing the poor had become a national sport!

3. *Sexual immorality was rife* (2:7b). Father and son used the same girl, i.e. prostitute, thus profaning the name of the Lord. This may or may not be temple prostitution, but it is, in this case cited, 'tantamount to incest, which according to the law, was to be punished with death (cf. Lev. 18:7,15; 20:11)'.[1]

4. *They profaned the worship of God* (2:8). They slept beside the altars – 'every altar', i.e., whether to Yahweh, as at Dan and Bethel, or pagan altars to Baal. They used as blankets garments taken as pledges for debts and which should have been returned to the poor man by nightfall (Exodus 22:26; Deuteronomy 24:12,13). They also caroused with wine exacted from the people by unjust fines. These were the ethics of hypocrisy at their very lowest.

---

[1]C.F. Keil and F. Delitzsch, *Commentary on the Old Testament* (Eerdmans), Vol. X (Minor Prophets), p.253.

Rejected love (2:9-12)

In sinning against God's law, Israel sinned against the grace of God. There is a modern tendency, even among professing Christians, to regard any insistence on the rigorous observance of law, even God's law, as essentially legalistic – that is, the mere keeping of arbitrary rules. It is as if all law is like the 30 m.p.h. speed limit – a sort of arbitrary but generally helpful guide-line, as long as it is not taken too seriously! Only an excessive breach of the rules could justify a rebuke. Rules, after all, are made to be broken! In this way, sexual immorality, as God has defined it, is softened to 'sowing wild oats' and a little bit of vandalism becomes 'youthful pranks'. Law that is insisted upon is then regarded as 'unfeeling' and 'too strict'. The God who insists upon complete obedience to his Word is viewed as a tyrant and a killjoy. The truth is, however, that God gave his law because of his *love* for his people. With the law, God sent great blessings that were designed to give them a happy life as a nation devoted to God and to be an encouragement to them to walk in his ways. At the centre of God's covenant with Israel was the divine love seeking the salvation of sinners – not some merely punctilious and impossible moral code that could only depress and repel real human beings. The loving purpose of God was for his people to experience the true happiness – holiness to the Lord. Law as the way of holiness is therefore the way of happiness and, rightly understood, is the expression of love – God's love to man and man's response of love to God (and men). For this reason, Amos reminds Israel of some instances of God's covenant love towards them – and their response.

1. The prophet reminds them that their whole history has been accompanied by God's loving presence with them. There is no evidence that God gave them an impossible standard to keep (the law) and then left them to fend for themselves. In fact, generation after generation experienced his love and mercy. God brought them out of Egypt (2:10) and gave them victory over the Canaanites (2:9).

2. He reminds them also that God sent them prophets to reveal God's will, to lead them to obedience and to tell of his

grace and his salvation. Moses, Joshua, Deborah, Samuel and many more, most of whose names are forgotten, testified to God's favour towards Israel. Furthermore, he raised up the Nazirite order (Numbers 6:2-21), men who, with their long hair and simple life-style, stood as a model of piety for the people as a whole.

What had been their response? **'But you made the Nazirites drink wine and commanded the prophets not to prophesy'** (2:12). The holiness of the former embarrassed them and the message of the latter offended them! They were a living reproach to the unclean lives of Israel's people! How many enthusiastic Christians today are coaxed and mocked into running with the world, doing what 'the boys' do? How many parents, who do not share the commitment to Christ of their child, tell him that 'It's a passing phase. When you're our age you'll realize that this is really extreme and unrealistic'? How many faithful ministers have been told by their congregations that they do not want to hear any more sermons on 'sin' and 'conversion'? Truth is never comfortable until it is embraced with a whole-hearted love for Christ. The lamentable reality is that the most virulent opposition to enthusiastic expressions of Christian commitment come from supposedly Christian people. Who wants today's prophets to tone down the message? Who would rather have 'gospel rock' than authoritative preaching of the Word? Surely the church, more than the world! The Word itself tells us that this will be the case. 'Even from your own number men will rise and distort the truth in order to draw away disciples after them' (Acts 20:30). It was God's people for whom the Lord Jesus wept, because they killed the prophets and stoned those sent to them (Matthew 23:37).

Covenantal justice (2:13-16)

No covenant is one-sided, in that, while the goal is to provide benefits for the parties, there will always be penalties for non-compliance with the terms of the agreement. Israel failed to keep covenant with God and so the penalties of covenant-breaking are invoked. They will be crushed **'as a cart crushes when loaded with grain'** (2:13). Strength, skill and swiftness will not save them. They are finished as a nation. So declares the Lord God.

This all seems so hopeless. But then, so did Jonah's prophecy against Nineveh, which was simply: 'Forty more days and Nineveh will be destroyed.' Was Nineveh destroyed? Was it not spared? And was it not because the people repented before the Lord? We must never lose sight of the fact that there is a silent call to repentance in every warning of divine judgement to come. Why? Because God's Word comes to men made in the image of God, men with a *sensus deitatis* – a creational awareness of God, men with consciences, however hardened by wickedness (Romans 2:15). The declaration of covenantal justice carries with it an echo of grace for sinners. This is more than an appeal to the natural fear with which everyone reacts to the threat of danger or pain. It is an appeal to the goodness of God and the awareness of that goodness of the Creator which is integral to the very constitution of man as the creature made in the image of God. To be sure, man the unbeliever, the rebel against God, suppresses that truth and sears his conscience and is in terrible danger of being given up to what God's Word calls a 'depraved' or 'reprobate mind' (Romans 1:18-32). But in wrath, God remembers mercy and calls all men everywhere to repent.

Israel, as it turned out, was finished and the ten tribes marched into exile and out of history, never to return. A valid and urgent application remains, however, for men and women, and for the church, and for all time. It is to hear the Word of God – to hear that your soul may live! (Isaiah 55:3.)

The primary focus of the message is, however, to the church. Are the various churches that call themselves 'Christian' any more faithful to God's Word than Israel was in Amos's day? Does God not have serious cause for controversy with the churches in this country? We do not need to detail the faithlessness of this denomination or that association. Mainline churches have a legendary capacity for fudging clearly-stated biblical teaching into inoffensive incomprehensibility and their Sunday services are empty to capacity. Many evangelicals, for all their zeal for scriptural orthodoxy, are often woefully attached to yesterday's battles and can be as lovelessly devoted to man-made traditions and forms as those whom they like to criticize. The Lord expects – and has an absolute and unconditional right to expect – that his professing people, the visible church upon earth, be faithful to his revealed Word in and through personal faith in his Son, the Lord Jesus Christ, as the once-for-all sacrifice for sin and King and Head of the church which is his body. 'You are my friends,' said Jesus, 'if you do what I command' (John 15:14). Do you hunger and thirst after righteousness? Do you delight in the law of the Lord? You may *feel* secure, even though such love for Christ is a closed book to you. They were secure on the mountain of Samaria as well! Meanwhile the devils tremble; they believe there is a God but that does not make them feel secure! (James 2:19.) Are you a Christian? Then here is God's Word for you: 'If we deliberately keep on sinning after we have received the knowledge of the truth, no sacrifice for sins is left, but only a fearful expectation of judgement and of raging fire that will consume the enemies of God. Anyone who rejected the law of Moses died without mercy on the testimony of two or three witnesses. How much more severely do you think a man deserves to be punished who has trampled the Son of God under foot, who has treated as an unholy thing the blood of the covenant that sanctified him, and who has insulted the Spirit of grace? For we know him who said, "It is mine to avenge; I will repay," and again, "The Lord will judge his people." It is a dreadful thing to fall into the hands of the living God.

Remember those earlier days after you had received the light, when you stood your ground in a great contest in the face of suffering. Sometimes you were publicly exposed to insult and persecution; at other times you stood side by side with those who were so treated. You sympathized with those in prison and joyfully accepted the confiscation of your property, because you knew that you yourselves had better and lasting possessions.

So do not throw away your confidence; it will be richly rewarded. You need to persevere so that when you have done the will of God, you will receive what he has promised. For in just a very little while,

> "He who is coming will come and not delay.
>   But my righteous one will live by faith.
> And if he shrinks back,
>   I will not be pleased with him."

But we are not of those who shrink back and are destroyed,
but of those who believe and are saved' (Hebrews 10:26-39).
May it be so with you!

Questions for study and discussion

1. Why is God particularly angry about covenant-breaking?
    (Read Luke 12:47,48; Hebrews 6:4-6.) What does this
    mean for Christians and the church in our day?
2. Distinguish between 'outward religion' and the inward
    experience of new life in Jesus Christ. (See Paul's
    expression 'inner being' in Ephesians 3:16.) Who can
    search the human heart? Is it possible for us to discern
    whether a person has genuine faith in Christ? (See
    Hebrews 4:12; Matthew 7:16; Romans 6:21,22; Galatians
    5:22; Jude 12.)
3. Discuss the meaning of the sins of Israel for the church
    today. Are there positions, officially held by particular
    churches, which are clearly opposed to God's Word? What
    does this mean for the ethics of individuals?
4. What was Israel's typical response to God's blessings? Is
    this evident in the churches of today? Where are the
    gospel's greatest enemies to be found? (Acts 20:30.)
5. What was to happen to Israel? What did happen? (See
    2 Kings 17:7-23.)
6. What ought our response to be? What ought to be the
    response of the churches? (John 15:14; Hebrews 10:26-39.)

3.
Leading questions

Please read Amos 3:1-8

Christians are often thought of as the irrational followers of an impossible way of life. Their faith is regarded as something a person either has or does not have. 'He's a "religious" person,' someone will say. It is as if that person's faith is a kind of congenital defect, a mystical syndrome he cannot help having, or, particularly if he has had a dramatic conversion to Christ, it is treated as a virus he has 'caught'!

In the popular mind there is a great divide between 'faith' and 'reason'. Modern man, unlike all his ancestors, is a post-Darwinian rationalist. The scientific method is, for him, the measure of what is rational and reasonable. Science 'proves' things, whereas everything else is just guessing or 'believing' on grounds that cannot be demonstrated by a scientific investigation. Science, very properly, can only deal with natural phenomena – what can be observed, handled and experimentally manipulated. It cannot, therefore, deal with the supernatural, which is, it is argued, inadmissible and invalid for any rational view of reality. This has been variously called the materialistic, naturalistic or scientistic (as distinct from scientific) world-view. The proper limits of science are taken as the definition of what is real and reasonable and true. Therefore God and his revealed Word are dismissed as having no positive relevance to the way men are to live or how they are to understand their world. God's Word and the Christian life then express, not absolute and eternal truth, but manifestations of man's intellectual evolution and expressions of his desire for security in an often hostile environment. For modern man, religion is an eccentricity which, to be sure, may be helpful to this individual or that on a personal basis, but in no way is to be considered fundamental, or even relevant, to the ordering of human society, the meaning of life or the goal of history, that is, the origin and the destiny of humanity.

It is to be expected, in such an atmosphere, that God's messengers will be regarded as irrational bigots who delight in calling down fire from heaven upon their largely unenthusiastic hearers. The absolutes of God's Word have never been welcome news to fallen mankind. If today secular humanism, based on scientistic-materialistic rejection of the claims of divine revelation, is the excuse for mocking God, in Israel of Amos's day it was the adoption of an easy religion, the tenets of which allowed all the latitude they needed to indulge their favourite sins. The very prosperity of their nation argued that God – Yahweh as redefined by the modern theologians in Dan and Bethel – approved of their current way of doing things and suggested strongly that Amos's old-fashioned fundamentalist God was dead. Those who sat at ease in Zion and felt secure on the mountains of Samaria (6:1) doubtless felt themselves to be men 'come of age' – liberated from the restrictiveness of the past and enjoying the fruits of their enlightened attitudes to national policy and personal ethics. They now had a 'balanced' view of the role of religion in modern life! Away with the prophets of doom!

A closer examination of God's message, however, shows that the Lord always addresses men as thinking, reasoning individuals. The Scriptures are not a pot-pourri of irrational invective and ecstatic emotionalism. There is no anti-intellectualism in the Bible's doctrine. God reveals his Word into history and argues his case with careful attention to the undeniable facts of human experience. Isaiah begins his prophecy with the passionate plea:

'Come now, let us reascn together,'
    says the LORD.
'Though your sins are like scarlet,
    they shall be white as snow;
though they are red like crimson,
    they shall be like wool.
If you are willing and obedient,
    you will eat the best from the land;
but if you resist and rebel,
    you will be devoured by the sword' (Isaiah 1:18-20).

'Let us reason together. Look at the arguments. Think through the Word of God as it relates to your real experience.' This is the challenge of the prophetic witness. Amos, in 3:1-8, gives a clear example of what the Lord called for in Isaiah 1:18-20. Israel is called to 'use its brains' and face up to reality by following through God's arguments a step at a time. They are thereby to convince themselves of the justice and holiness of God's dealings with them. This is always the method of God's Word. It was Jesus' method, for example, with the woman of Samaria and the rich young man (John 4:1-26; Mark 10:17-22). In both cases he led their reasoning in such a way that they had no alternative but to admit the truth. One went away rejoicing and the other sorrowful, but they both knew where they stood because it had been demonstrated irrefutably to their own minds. The power of God's Word to convince men and women of its truth is not in any emotionalism of its appeal, but in the reasonableness of its argument. There must be passion in the preaching of the Word of God and there cannot but be the stirring of the emotions in the hearing of both the warnings of the Scriptures and the message of salvation by free grace in Jesus Christ – it is after all a message concerning life and death both in time and eternity! It is truth grasped in the mind that moves us, on the one hand to rejoice with 'an inexpressible and glorious joy', or, on the other hand, to be 'furious' (1 Peter 1:8; Luke 4:28). The former embraces the truth in faith; the latter rejects it in unbelief. Amos argues a case in order to convince thinking people. Consequently he first re-emphasizes the accountability of the children of Israel before God (3:1,2), then goes on to ask some leading questions bearing upon God's dealings with them (3:3-6) and, finally, draws some conclusions relative to their response to God's Word (3:7,8).

Accountable to God (3:1,2)

The judgements announced upon Judah and Israel surely left them in no doubt as to their accountability to God. Their history was bound up in covenant with God and they had broken that covenant, an agreement into which they had entered willingly and solemnly (2:4-16).

In 3:1,2 God addresses the whole family of Israel, that is, both Israel (Samaria) and Judah. We might say that he speaks to the whole church, rather than one denomination. How easy it is for one denomination to slate other denominations for their sins! Judah might well have taken perverse pleasure in hearing the more severe judgements against Israel. There is always a great temptation to what the Germans call *'Schadenfreude'* – the enjoyment of the miseries of others. This is an effective way of giving oneself a back-handed compliment ('I am not as bad as he is!') and it is one of the most common ways of avoiding the implications of one's own sins. But God will have none of this. So he removes, at a stroke, even the slightest pretext for explaining away the comprehensiveness of his claims. He who thinks he is standing firm, let him be careful that he doesn't fall (1 Corinthians 10:12).

1.   **'You only have I chosen of all the families of the earth'** (3:2a). The word translated 'chosen' (the Hebrew *yāda'*) is more commonly rendered 'known' in the Old Testament. God's choice, or election, of his people is certainly included in this verb, but the heart of its meaning is the particularity of God's gracious knowledge of those whom he plans to save. He *knows* them with that intimacy of involvement in which he surrounded them with his favour and led them in covenant faithfulness, generation after generation. They were his people – loved, called and chosen – his church, 'the council of the holy ones' (Psalm 89:7); 'the pillar and foundation of the truth' (1 Timothy 3:15). The obvious is not mentioned – they have squandered this blessing and exhausted the patience of God. The reckoning is at hand.

2.   **'Therefore I will punish you for all your sins'** (3:2b). This was something that should have come as no surprise to Israel, for it was the clear provision of the law in the case of outright rejection of God's Word (Leviticus 26:14-33).

Seven leading questions (3:3-6)

The point is now driven home in a series of questions. Like a skilful interrogator, the Lord leads the interviewed nation to see her true condition. These questions have no recorded answers because the answers are obvious. There is no escaping the awful realities of the situation! This is the searcher of hearts at work. What a model it provides for Christian preaching! The message goes straight to the heart of the matter, allowing no opportunity to wriggle out from under God's claims.

Ultimately, all the questions lead to the answer to one vital question, namely, 'Is God being fair, to bring such judgements?' Men will always protest that, whatever their actual shortcomings, these are not bad enough to justify the censure or sentence being imposed upon them. An illuminating instance of this is recorded in Malachi 2:17-3:15. There, in the face of judgement, the wicked profess to have no idea why it is that the Lord is weary with their words (2:17), their robbery of his tithes (3:8) and their opposition (3:13) and it falls to the prophet to spell out the answer in no uncertain terms. There is no mitigation of the offence – only the necessity for repentance or judgement.

1. **'Do two walk together unless they have agreed to do so?'** (3:3) If you fall out with a friend and there is no reconciliation, would you still socialize in the same old way? Of course not! You cannot just go on as if nothing has happened. There is a cause and an effect. So it is between Israel and her God. The wonder – and it is a wonder of grace in the long-suffering attitude of God towards sinners – is that the parting of the ways had not come sooner. Is God justified in making the break with Israel? 'Think, Israel,' Amos is saying, 'and you must see that friendship is built on agreement and faithfulness. Why, then, can you not admit that the Lord has a right to be annoyed with you?' God is just in his judgements (Psalm 19:9).

2. **'Does a lion roar in the thicket when he has no prey?'** (3:4a) Amos challenges their reading of the signs of the times. The lion is roaring. Lions do not roar when the prey has the possibility of escape. In other words, Israel ought not to indulge the thought that it cannot happen to them! The very ministry of the prophet ought to tell them that the threat is not idle. When the policeman arrests the criminal, the game is up!

3. **'Does he growl in his den when he has caught nothing?'** (3:4b) He growls because he is already devouring his prey! Israel is 'condemned already' (compare John 3:18)

and the evidence of the fulfilment of God's judgements is there
to be seen for the discerning eye. Israel feels secure, but the
things she supposes are blessings are devouring her – a word
indeed for the 'consumer society' in our own century!

4.   **'Does a bird fall into a trap on the ground where no
snare has been set?'** (3:5a) Here is the idea of temptation.
Israel went for the bait and is ensnared in the trap of spiritual
and moral evil. Birds do not get caught in unset traps. Israel
saw sin as attractive and threw herself into it, knowing that she
was turning from God.

5.   **'Does a trap spring up from the earth when there is
nothing to catch?'** (3:5b) What does the springing of a trap
show? That the prey has been caught red-handed! The
prophetic word, in other words, points up the guilt of Israel.
The calamities coming upon the nation are the evidence of
their culpability and they have no right to be surprised at
God's reaction! The writing is on the wall. They are weighed in
the balance and found wanting!

6.   **'When a trumpet sounds in a city, do not the people
tremble?'** (3:6a) Think now of the effect of judgement. The
approach of danger puts the fear of death into men. Yet Israel
is not trembling! 'Even the demons believe . . . – and shudder,'
said James (James 2:19). They know the truth in their own
way and are more realistic than men, who will go on dreaming
that it cannot happen to them. The contemporary application
is clear. The modern church, steeped in its comfortable
conviction of universal salvation by the moral influence of the
good example of a man named Jesus (who was never born of a
virgin, true God and true man, and never died as a
substitutionary, atoning sacrifice for sinners and never
actually rose from the dead on the third day) is just like Israel
of old. Has she not replaced the substance of biblical faith with
a mere form of words that sounds a bit like the original but is,
in effect, a new religion of human invention? God's trumpet is
sounding for theological liberalism, but are the people
trembling?

7.   **'When disaster comes to a city, has not the Lord
caused it?'** (3:6b) God cannot be mocked (Galatians 6:7). He is
certainly not 'an arbitrary tyrant who destroys for the sheer

lust of murder'.[1] He is a God of mercy as well as justice. He had issued repeated warnings and these had gone unheeded. The axe must now be laid to the root of the tree. He who maintains love for thousands will by no means leave the guilty unpunished! Again, the question concerns reading the signs of the times and accepting that they have a case to answer before God.

Our whole history – whether we are thinking of our individual experiences or the broader scope of national history – is rightly understood only when we see it as God's providence. History is the unfolding of God's purpose for man, at every level of experience – from individual to national and on to the international and universal history of humanity. This includes both good experiences and bad, although in an obviously wicked world it is the latter that tend to come to the fore. From the whole complex of blessing and curse we can learn of the goodness and severity of God. Personal and national calamities should trouble human consciences and engender deep self-examination and a seeking of God's Scripture-revealed will for both personal and national life. National 'days of prayer' ought to be characterized by such a brokenness of spirit, just as, on the other side of God's dealings, observances of national thanksgiving – perhaps for the harvest, or deliverance in war – ought to be the occasion of quiet and humble gratitude for God's mercies. The question many ask, in the face of tragedy, is 'Why?' or 'Why me?' And, sadly, this is where the questioning ends – or ends endlessly in a mantra-like repetition into the void – 'Why? . . . Why? . . . Why? . . .' with no answer sought beyond the eternal echo of self-pity. The answer to the question 'Why?' is at one level obvious and at another inscrutable. It is obvious at the simple level of the fact of sin in the heart of man. It reminds me that I am a sinner who must give account to God. All human tragedy teaches this plain fact. Yet this is what the unconverted sinner wants to avoid facing, for it would require him to face the question of his need of a Saviour. He would have to admit that he was lost and deserved not only such disasters as he had observed or experienced, but also eternal condemnation away from God for

---

[1]T. Laetsch *The Minor Prophets* (Concordia, 1956), p.150.

ever in what Scripture calls hell! At another level, calamities
are inscrutable just because it is impossible to make a detailed
link between cause and effect – to say, for example, that this
particular sin occasioned that particular judgement. Indeed,
there are no doubt very few, if any, instances in which such a
connection can be made and it is surely unprofitable to
speculate about such matters. It is enough that all calamities
make us think about God's claims upon our lives and that this
leads us to approach him with a broken spirit and a contrite
heart, seeking his blessing in and through the shed blood of his
Son, the Lord Jesus Christ, the only Redeemer of men! The
questions 'Why?' and 'Why me?' ought to be answered
immediately with an inner awareness of personal sin and guilt
before God, to be followed by a second question: 'What must I
do to be saved?' and a third: 'What shall I do, Lord?' This, of
necessity, brings us to the Word of God and the threshold of a
renewed life. The jailer in Philippi saw the finger of God in the
earthquake and the release of the prisoners' chains. If they
escaped, he was as good as dead. So he prepared to kill himself,
but was restrained by Paul's assurance that they were all there.
The calamity turned into an occasion of candid self-
examination and he was converted to Christ and found new life
in him (Acts 16:22-34). This is the real answer to all the
temporal judgements of God. 'Seek the Lord while he may yet
be found. Call on him while he is near' (Isaiah 55:6).

Clear warning (3:7,8)

It is often forgotten that the element of warning is an essential
component of the gospel ministry. Sin and judgement to come
are not popular subjects today. The preaching of God's law has
taken a back seat to endless disquisitions on 'how to' be a better
Christian, a better mother or a better . . . whatever. Hell is a
forgotten doctrine and even heaven has been moved to this side
of eternity – no doubt to accommodate the expectations of the
latter-day perfectionists of the 'how-to' school of Christian
living. There is a grave imbalance in Christian preaching and
personal witnessing when the gospel is presented more as a

means of personal improvement, even of 'mind cure',[2] than as good news of a full salvation from the wrath of God against sin and from the guilt and corruption of sin both now and in eternity. Is it, perhaps, symptomatic of the confusion and doctrinal illiteracy of the modern church, that a godly pastor, in a thoroughly evangelical denomination, engaged in an exposition of the Ten Commandments, can be the subject of a complaint to the governing body of his denomination that he preached too much on sin, had 'banished love from the congregation' and never preached on texts teaching the love of Christ, such as 'Jesus loves me, this I know'?[3] This extreme case is mirrored, in a milder way, by that prevalent aversion in the modern church to the careful definition of biblical holiness and of the consequences – temporal and eternal – of practical ungodliness. Amos *warned* Israel of God's plan and purpose. He did so in the plainest of language. Through the prophets God revealed his plans. He did nothing without so revealing his purpose (3:7). This is the meaning of the ministry of God's Word in every age.

Now you may choose not to listen; you may go to other, more comfortable, preachers; you may even do your best to silence God's messengers (7:12); but when the Day of the Lord comes, you are going to remember the faithful preacher and that message you so earnestly detested! Then the false teachers who told you what you wanted to hear will be seen in perspective – God's perspective – and you will live with that false teaching in the second death of a lost eternity (Revelation 21:8).

> 'Come now, let us reason together . . .
> Though your sins are like scarlet,
>   they shall be white as snow'
> $\qquad\qquad\qquad\qquad$ (Isaiah 1:18).

'Turn! Turn from your evil ways! Why will you die, O house of Israel?' (Ezekiel 33:11.)

---

[2] For an illuminating treatment of this theme, see Donald Meyer, *The Positive Thinkers*, (Pantheon, New York: 1980).

[3] The 'text' in question is, you will have noticed, from a well-known hymn and not from the Bible.

The final word (3:8) shows the intimate relationship between God's Word and human response. When he speaks, those who hear him in faith 'can but prophesy'. Amos was given direct revelation of predictive prophecy and has a certain uniqueness in his ministry, which cannot be duplicated by any other. We have the completed Scriptures of the Old and New Testaments and our privilege is to minister these truths already given to the church under the inspiration of God. Who can but prophesy? It is our prophetic task – that of the New Testament church – to witness to the glory of the Saviour and tell the world of his way of salvation. We must warn men to flee the wrath to come and urge them to believe on the Lord Jesus Christ that they might have eternal life. The claims of the lordship of Jesus Christ must be pressed upon individuals and nations alike, and the judgements of the living God upon unrepentant reprobate sinners must be declared with tears and pleadings, for the wicked shall be condemned to hell (Psalm 9:17; Matthew 23:33; 2 Peter 2:4-9).

Believe on the Lord Jesus Christ and you will be saved.

Questions for study and discussion

1. Discuss Leviticus 26:14-33 in relation to God's particular judgements against the apostasy of the covenant people. What does this imply for the church today?
2. What are believers meant to be like? (Exodus 19:5; Galatians 5:13-26; 1 Peter 2:4-12.)
3. Discuss God's reasoning with Israel in Amos 3:3-6. Is the Christian faith rational, or merely subjective and emotional? Read Peter's sermons in Acts 2:14-40 and 3:11-26; Stephen's, Acts 7:2-53; and Paul's, Acts 13:16-41; 17:22-31. Are these appeals to the emotions only, or even principally?
4. What is the only reason for witnessing to God's truth? How does God speak to us today? How can man and God walk together?
5. Discuss the preaching of judgement in the work of the gospel of Christ.

4.
The naked truth

Please read Amos 3:9-15

Everyone knows the story of the emperor's new clothes. He is persuaded that he has the finest of clothes, but his fawning courtiers are afraid to tell him the truth. So on the great day of the parade it falls to a little boy to point out to the embarrassment of all that the emperor actually has no clothes at all!

This perfectly illustrates the thrust of Amos 3:9-15. The heathen nations witness the nakedness of Israel's self-deceit and false security. Like the Laodicean church eight centuries later, Israel thinks herself rich and wealthy, having need of nothing, when in truth she is 'wretched, pitiful, poor, blind and naked' (Revelation 3:17). 'All that glisters is not gold,' as the Bard of Avon asserted. Through the prophet, we see Israel from heaven's windows. We see Israel as others see her and we are given a lesson in the vital matter of self-knowledge, as opposed to self-deceit. The true knowledge of self is, of course, God's knowledge of who we really are and God's interpretation of what is right and what is wrong in our lives. And what is said of Israel casts its applicatory shadow over the church.

The prophet resolves his message into three distinct points. First of all, he shows that the sin of God's people will be exposed to the world (3:9,10); secondly, he points out that the remnant that is spared will stand as a witness to the chastisement of his people (3:11,12) and, thirdly, he affirms that the world is used by God to destroy the backslidden covenant nation (3:13-15). The general application throughout, as has been noted already in these studies, is to the church – the visible, professing church of Jesus Christ – in the present age.

49

The watching world (3:9,10)

Amos sketches an imaginary scene in which heralds are sent
out to proclaim the sins of Israel, as it were, from the house-
tops. Egypt and Philistia, perhaps the two greatest oppressors
of God's people, are called to Samaria to witness Israel's
decadence: **'See the great unrest within her and the
oppression among her people'** (3:9). They will see that
Israelite society is incapable of doing what is right, so eroded is
the moral sense of the nation. They will see the mad
acquisitiveness of an unjust and degraded culture (3:10). Even
the heathen will be amazed at the spectacle!

The point is that the wickedness of God's people has
surpassed that of the heathen and is now an abomination in
God's sight, and the seal of this fact is that the heathen nations
shall be witnesses against them. What a desperate irony this is!
Those to whom Israel ought to have borne witness concerning
the righteousness of God now become witnesses of her
apostasy!

Israel is a portion of the church of the Old Testament
period. Her behaviour – and God's reaction to that behaviour
– speaks powerfully to the modern church and to every
professing Christian. Perhaps three significant truths stand out
as having the most pointed application to the current scene.

1.   The church has been created by God to be the bearer of the
light of the gospel of Christ in the world. She is to preach Christ
as a Saviour with every word and every action. Every believer
is to preach Christ and be a living example of what Jesus can
do to turn a sinner into a new creation, for, as the apostle Paul
has written, 'If anyone is in Christ, he is a new creation; the old
has gone, the new has come!' (2 Corinthians 5:17.) The church
is God's chosen instrument to seek the lost and point them to
Christ. In her preaching and witness his light shines before
men. Fed by the oil of the Holy Spirit, the lampstands – the
churches constituting the whole church in the world – shine
forth the light of the Word, even as Christ stands in the midst of
them (Revelation 1:12-2:1). Israel was to be a light to the
nations. They were to observe God's law carefully, for this
would show their wisdom and understanding to the nations

(Deuteronomy 4:5-8). The heathen would then testify to that wisdom. So also is the church of the New Testament to spread the Word by a godly witness: 'You are the light of the world . . . let your light shine before men, that they may see your good deeds and praise your Father in heaven' (Matthew 5:14,16). 'Be imitators of God . . . as dearly loved children and live a life of love, just as Christ loved us and gave himself up for us as a fragrant offering and sacrifice to God' (Ephesians 5:1). You – the church, Christians – are the light of the world! Be that light in the only way possible – in practical obedience to Christ Jesus, the only Saviour of men and women.

2.   The world is watching the church. The world expects Christians to practise what they preach – or what they ought to preach! The world expects Christians to maintain a higher level of morality, humility and piety than it would ever dream of aspiring to itself. This is not hypocrisy; it is simply taking Christians at their word! Yes, the unbelieving folk around you, Christian friend, expect you to have 'a holier life' and 'a more sensitive conscience'![1] They would love to be able to poke a little fun at the inconsistent Christian. But, on the serious side, this would provide an excuse for shrugging off the claims of Christ.

No doubt some Christians complain about such a state of affairs. It seems unfair. So what? The world must be expected to be unfair. It is a *fallen* world, after all! If, however, you claim to follow Christ and your life is as worldly as the next man's, why should anyone listen to you when you say he needs a Saviour who will forgive his sins and give him a new life? God says that 'Faith without works is dead' (James 2:20, AV). Dead faith does not impress anybody. It is just a lot of words! And all that achieves is to devalue the Christian gospel in the eyes of the world. If all that the gospel means is an *unchanged* life plus a lot of righteous words, then who needs it? And what does that say about Christ's power to change? No, the unchanged Christian is a contradiction in terms! He is a pretend Christian whose 'witness' is an anti-witness that points people *away* from

---

[1] H. Veldkamp, *The Farmer from Tekoa*, (Paideia: 1977), p.111.

Christ. He is a stumbling-block preventing sinners from coming to Christ.

There is no other witness to Christ, in fact, than the witness of humbled, repentant believers, who confess their sins and hypocrisies and seek the enabling grace of God to do his will. 'For,' says the apostle Paul to the Ephesians, 'we are God's workmanship, created in Christ Jesus to do good works, which God prepared in advance for us to do' (Ephesians 2:10). When Israel saw the heathen observing her wickedness, she should have been overwhelmed with shame and guilt and fled to God in faith and repentance. All she did was have another round of drinks! (4:1.)

3. There is a peculiar vileness to the sins of those who say they belong to Christ but deny it by their actions. Churches are legendary for the virulence of their disputes and notorious for their vindictive treatment of their own minorities. The American atheist, Madalyn Murray O'Hair, once said that what distinguished Christians from the rest of the world was that Christians 'killed their own wounded'. This is, of course, a bare-faced slander rooted in her well-known hatred for the gospel. The claims of Christ are well enough known, even by atheists, to make it clear that his will is that true brotherly love should characterize all the behaviour of believers. Anyone who hates his brother, says the Bible, is a murderer and does not have eternal life in him (1 John 3:15). Cases of church discipline are to be conducted with the utmost graciousness, in order to achieve the restoration of the offender (Matthew 18:15-20; 1 Corinthians 5:1-5; 2 Corinthians 2:5-11). Nevertheless, the failures of Christians and churches to observe these clear teachings of the Scriptures beg a very solemn question: are we seeing *real* Christians in action? In Israel's case, the answer is clear: outwardly they were God's people, but inwardly they were thoroughly wicked. As Paul wrote, so many years later, 'A man is not a Jew if he is only one outwardly, nor is circumcision merely outward and physical. No, a man is a Jew if he is one inwardly; and circumcision is circumcision of the heart, by the Spirit, not by the written code. Such a man's praise is not from men, but from God' (Romans 2:28,29).

This is for the conscience of every Christian. Israel seared her conscience and went down to destruction. What about you?

A piece of an ear (3:11,12)

Hitherto the Lord has addressed the Egyptians and the Philistines. Now, his attention turns to Israel. Destruction will overcome the land. The enemy will pull down her strongholds and plunder her fortresses (3:11). It is as if God is saying, 'Yes, I know you have secure borders, large armies and a high standard of living! But, for your sins, all this will dissolve in blood and ruin! You may not listen to the prophets of the living God, but you *will* pay attention to the swords of your heathen conquerors!'

The scope of the disaster is, paradoxically, highlighted by the remnant that will be spared. Just as the shepherd rescued **'only two leg bones'** or **'a piece of an ear'** from a sheep taken by a lion, so Israel would have left to them **'the edge of their beds'** and **'the corner of their couches'** (3:12).

Why does the prophet compare Israel's catastrophe with the pieces of a sheep retrieved by the shepherd? In Exodus 22:13 there is a provision for a man who has lost an animal entrusted to his care by a neighbour (lost it, that is, to a wild animal) to 'bring the remains as evidence' so that he would not have to pay compensation to the owner. He was thereby cleared of any suspicion that he had sold the animal. The meaning, for Israel's demise as a nation, is that God, the Shepherd of Israel, is clear of any negligence in the matter of the destruction of his erstwhile sheep at the hands of their enemies. They have brought this destruction upon themselves.

The salvation of a remnant has a threefold significance that is central to any understanding of God's *plan of redemption*. This may seem a strange thing to say in the context of Israel's destruction. Yet it remains a fact that God's ultimate purpose in all of his dealings with men is to save his people from their sins.

1. The remnant is a witness to the justice of God's judgements upon the wicked. God is perfectly righteous in his actions. He refines and cleanses his church; he clothes her with the character of a 'remnant' – humbled, gentle, dependent upon his grace, weak in the eyes of the world yet strong in faith, hope and love – and in this way he all the more demonstrates to the world the justice of his cause and kingdom.

2. The remnant witnesses to the faithfulness of the great Shepherd of the sheep (Psalm 23:1; 80:1) who has promised never to forsake his people. Ezra, in his beautiful prayer for the backslidings of the returned exiles from Babylon, gave expression to this thought: 'But now, for a brief moment, the Lord our God has been gracious in leaving us a remnant and giving us a firm place in his sanctuary, and so our God gives light to our eyes and a little relief in our bondage' (Ezra 9:8). 'Unless the Lord Almighty had left us some survivors,' cried Isaiah, 'we would have become like Sodom, we would have been like Gomorrah' (Isaiah 1:9). The remnant is proof of his abiding love in the face of human rebellion.

3. The remnant witnesses to the future completion of the work of redemption. God's people shall multiply as the sands of the sea-shore (Genesis 22:17). The final state of the church in heaven is 'a great multitude that no one could count' (Revelation 7:9). The church will be a multiplying 'remnant' – always a remnant, but constantly gathering in men and women until she becomes the 'general assembly and church of the first-born' of Jesus Christ (Hebrews 12:22,23, AV). Here is glorious encouragement! Here is the victory of the cross of Christ come into its own!

The scourge of God (3:13-15)

God turns again to the heathen nations. They are to testify against the house of Jacob (3:13). They are to pronounce the judgement and to see that it is executed! They, like Attila and the Huns in the last days of the Roman Empire, are to be the 'scourge of God' upon a rotten culture! The terms of that punishment are comprehensive. The false religion, with its altars at Dan and Bethel, will be swept away (3:14), while the fancy houses of the affluent will be reduced to ashes (3:15). Even the **'horns of the altar'** – the symbols of mercy, to which the guilty might cling (1 Kings 1:50-53; 2:28-34) and between which burnt offerings were made and the blood of sacrifice for sin smeared – all would be no more. No more mercy; no more grace for the nation – indeed, no more nation!

This is more than the account of the end of a little kingdom in the Near East; it is a perspective upon history itself! What is the real meaning of the rise and fall of nations? The Bible says that 'Righteousness exalts a nation, but sin is a disgrace to any people' (Proverbs 14:34). Is it a political question? Or an economic question? Is it a demographic or an ethnic phenomenon? Or a combination of any or all of these factors? Can any such factors be abstracted from the consideration of God's sovereignty over history and the execution of his just judgements *and*, not least, his plan of redemption through the death of his only begotten Son, the Lord Jesus Christ? As far as secular-humanist historians are concerned, God is not even a spectator of the progress of the human race. He is a 'factor' in history only in so far as the subjective religious notions of men have affected their behaviour. Karl Marx, for example, saw religion as the 'opium of the people' – significant, to be sure, but essentially a psychologistic phantasm wonderfully adapted to exploiting the masses. God's Word knows nothing of such a view-point, although Scripture might well agree that false religion is a kind of 'opium' with which men and women anaesthetize themselves against the conscience-piercing claims of Jesus Christ. Scripture makes clear that the deeper meaning of the movements of history is to be found in the revealed truth that God is sovereign and that, in the New Testament era, the Lord Jesus Christ exercises his messianic kingship over all things (Ephesians 1:20-23; 1 Corinthians 15:24; Hebrews 1:3; 8:1; Revelation 11:15). 'All authority in heaven and on earth has been given to me,' declares the Lord Jesus Christ (Matthew 28:18). This is the bedrock of the Christian understanding of history and, ultimately, the reason for the believer's confidence and contentment in the midst of an often hostile and confusing world.

Amos shows us that God has a controversy with men. Furthermore, as the prophet Daniel was later to declare,

'He does as he pleases with the powers of heaven
    and the peoples of the earth.
No one can hold back his hand
    or say to him: "What have you done?"'

(Daniel 4:35).

God used the heathen nations to purge the kingdom of Israel. He would later use Cyrus, King of Persia, to restore the Jews to Jerusalem and even calls that heathen king 'my shepherd' (Isaiah 44:28). Let the modern church – for it is to the church that the message of Amos is principally directed – face God's realities! Why should God not sweep away the nations of the West, with their churches that believe everything but the plain teaching of God's Word, and therefore believe nothing? Why should our pseudo-Christian culture, with its mindless worship of the 'standard of living' and endless obsession with sensual pleasure, be any more durable than that of Israel? What is the remedy? Israel was called to repentance, albeit in the context of a declaration of imminent destruction. Likewise, modern man is called to repentance, though it is in the context of the accomplishment of salvation for sinners by the risen Christ! The message comes first to the church, for judgement must begin at the house of God (1 Peter 4:17), but extends to the whole society of men. Do not imagine that your present safety, compared, say, with the distinct lack of security of so many elsewhere in the world, means that they are more guilty sinners than you. Jesus asked the Jews if they thought that the eighteen who died in the collapse of the tower in Siloam were more guilty than the others living in Jerusalem at the time. His answer was 'I tell you, no! But unless you repent, you too will all perish' (Luke 13:1-5).

Questions for study and discussion

1. Why does God so expose and humiliate the professing church before the world? (See Revelation 3:17; Luke 16:8.)
2. What was Israel's sin as described in 3:9,10? What is the problem with the sins of Christians? What is God concerned about? (Romans 2:28,29; Ephesians 2:20; compare Matthew 5:14-16; Ephesians 5:1.)
3. Read Romans 11:5. What does the 'piece of an ear' tell us about God's plan for the church? Compare Ezra 9:8; Isaiah 1:9; Romans 11:5 with Genesis 22:17; Hebrews 12:22,23; Revelation 7:9.
4. Can you see ways, in modern times, or in past history, where God has used the 'world' to chastise, purge and refine the church? Compare what is happening to the church in the West and in Communist countries like Russia and China.
5. What positive response is God calling for in our day?

5.
The cows of Bashan

Please read Amos 4:1-5

Nicknames have a long but not always honourable history. At its best, however, such 'name-calling' is cleverly descriptive and perhaps even affectionate. We can all remember teachers from our schooldays by their nicknames. I think of my English teacher, 'Bouncer' – so called because his name, Stott, sounds like 'stot', the Scottish word for 'bounce'!

God's Word uses nicknames from time to time – not for fun or abuse, but to describe and to illustrate something about the person concerned. And the Lord chooses his words with infinite care. Herod, for example, is 'that fox' (Luke 13:32). The Lord Jesus Christ describes himself, in the language of prophecy, as 'a worm and not a man' (Psalm 22:6). James and John, the Lord's disciples, were nicknamed 'Boanerges', which means 'the sons of thunder' – a reference to their passionate zeal as disciples (Mark 3:17). This is the language of divine inspiration. These are not 'throw-away' remarks. They are in Scripture to instruct us, not merely to give colour to the text. This is no less the case when Amos speaks to the women of Israel and addresses them: '. . . you cows of Bashan'. He means to make a serious point about their behaviour, as we shall see. He is not at all interested in hurling abuse at them. It is to inform and, hopefully, to reform that such language is used. Interestingly, a similar expression is used of the male gender in Psalm 22:11. There, wicked men are called 'strong bulls of Bashan'. This tells us of the self-confidence, arrogance and strength of those who oppose the Messiah and thereby expresses something of the righteous anger of the Lord against their wickedness.

In the context of Amos's prophecy, the naming of the society wives as 'cows of Bashan' ought to be heard with seriousness – indeed, with conviction of sin. Amos is speaking most earnestly to the cultured despisers of the God of Israel. He is not sneering at them. He is not using the language of the gutter. He is highlighting the causes of God's anger with this particular class of people in Israel.

The love of luxury (4:1)

The contribution of the women to Israel's condition now comes into view. They are called 'cows' – not a flattering description for the fine ladies of Samaria! This is not, as in modern British slang, because they are promiscuous and uncultured. They are 'cows *of Bashan*', a reference to the fine cattle from the rich pastureland of Bashan. They – the ladies – are sleek and well-fed! They are utterly materialistic! They never stop 'chewing the cud' of luxury! They must have more . . . and more . . . and more . . . and they are quite prepared to oppress the poor and crush the needy to satisfy their desires. They share the goals of their husbands, namely, to have a life of ease and financial security. Like them, they are morally and spiritually bankrupt; they will trample on the 'little man' to gain their ends. They love luxury, hence the appellation 'cows of Bashan'.

How did these wives oppress the poor? Almost certainly, they would not have done so directly. The Israelite wife would very likely be very much 'behind the scenes', away from public view. But she would be very influential none the less – perhaps even the 'power behind the throne'. Amos only says that they said to their husbands, 'Bring us some drinks!' They let their husbands know what would please them and, as is so often the case today, it is excessive drinking that stands as the badge of the insatiable appetite of the voluptuary.

This affords at least three points of general application to the way we are to think about sin and guilt.

1. *Sin is always more a matter of the heart than the hand.* The husbands may do the actual exploiting, while the wives plot, plan and promote the whole sorry business from behind the scenes. If the men commit the 'sins of the hand', the women are

equally guilty of the root-cause of these actions – the sins of the heart committed to avarice and pleasure. As a man thinks in his heart, so is he (Proverbs 23:7, AV). The same is to be said of the ladies!

2.   *Formal outward correctness can exist when inward integrity has been destroyed.* Our English text says that these women said to their **'husbands, "Bring us some drinks!"'** (4:1) The Hebrew word for 'husbands' is literally 'lords'. These wives, in other words, used the language of Sarah towards Abraham (Genesis 18:12; 1 Peter 3:6) without any evidence of Sarah's godliness. There is outward form – the language of piety – without any inner commitment to God's will. Why do we say this? Because God's will for a wife is submissiveness to her husband (Ephesians 5:22) with the proviso that God's Word be paramount in the relationship. If anything, these wives ought to have opposed their husbands' schemes rather than aid and abet them! Calling a man 'lord' is one thing, but encouraging him to be God's kind of 'lord' is something else again.

3.   *There is such a thing as complicity in error.* The wife who never personally prosecuted one of the poor before the judge shares her husband's guilt because she is his accomplice. One may pull the trigger, but all are guilty of the crime – not excluding the driver of the get-away car! Achan hid stolen goods in the earth under his tent and this involved the complicity of his family (Joshua 7:24,25). The tribe of Benjamin was punished for its complicity in the rape-murder of the Levite's concubine by the men of Gibeah (Judges 19-20). Indeed, the whole community ('society' in modern parlance) was held, in a certain sense, to be responsible in the case of the unsolved murder of a man (Deuteronomy 21:1-9). In this case, the guilt of the community was not for the murder itself, but for the justice that could not be executed on the guilty party. Corporate responsibility, in the face of the sin of an individual, is to see that justice is done. This holds for the family and the church as for the wider community, even the nation. Not to dissent from, say, the sinful policy of a government or not to bear witness to the sin of a wayward son is to share, in a measure, their guilt. The 'cows of Bashan' not only did not

dissent from their husbands' activities, but positively egged them on to greater excesses!

There is also a sidelight in our text on what happens when the marriage relationship becomes a seed-bed for wickedness. Marriage is, as many Christian rubrics have it, for 'mutual help in godly living'. It is not designed to destroy and oppress society or the individuals within the marriage covenant. We do not recognize the graces of Ephesians 5:22-33 and 1 Peter 3:1-7 in the ruling-class marriages of Samaria. The respective roles of husband and wife are perverted and the home serves Mammon rather than God. The basic point is that in marriage, as in every aspect of life, we come face to face with the Bible's doctrine of *antithesis* – the opposition between light and darkness, between Christ and the devil, between God's way and man's way! The challenge is to bring all our thoughts and actions, all our ambitions and relationships into captivity to Christ. 'Make me a captive, Lord, and then I shall be free!' – free to be God's man or God's woman or God's family!

The punishment fits the crime (4:2,3)

The Lord is explicit as to the judgement to follow.

'**The Sovereign Lord has sworn by his holiness**' (4:2). The Lord takes this oath in his own name, 'since there was no one greater for him to swear by' (Hebrews 6:13). This 'puts an end to all argument' (Hebrews 6:16).

They will be **'taken away with hooks ... with fish-hooks'**. The 'cows of Bashan' are now seen as fish. Israel is a fish-pond and Assyria is the angler. A sidelight on this is afforded by a memorial stone, the Senjirli Stele. This commemorates the victory of the Assyrian king, Esarhaddon, over the Egyptians. Esarhaddon is shown holding cords that are attached to the lips of captive kings! The subjugated peoples are dragged away, like fish on an angler's line! The 'cows of Bashan' will be taken **'through breaks in the wall'** and **'cast out towards Harmon'** – possibly a reference to exile in Armenia (4:3).

True churchianity (4:4,5)

We must not think of the 'cows of Bashan' as out-and-out, openly, grossly wicked people. They were normal people, albeit people with wealth and position in society. They were, to be sure, the people 'on the make' – the 'movers and shakers' in society and the 'hangers-on', the social climbers and the entrepreneurs, that is to say, the 'successful' people, who have 'made something of their lives'. They were the kind of people that most people want to be, if only they could have the opportunity! And they go to church! They were pillars of the church. They were quite keen on the observance of the regular forms of religious worship. They brought sacrifices and gave free-will offerings. And like so many of us, their religion had very little to do with their daily lives. It did, perhaps, provide the comfort of knowing that they had 'done their bit' for God, while letting them get on with the business of succeeding in life, unfettered by any necessity to take seriously the ethics of old-fashioned theology or narrow-minded prophets!

This, in modern terms, is the 'churchianity' that is the bane of church life in the 'cow of Bashan' culture of the consumer society of the West. Outward form. A pound coin in the plate. A barely whispered hymn. 'What *is* the preacher on about today?' Gloves on during the benediction. Click of handbags. 'Nice to see you, Mrs Jones. Yes, it's been a while. August, wasn't it? Oh, your family is here for Christmas . . . Must hurry . . . 'Bye.'

Churchianity is not something that affects 'them' rather than 'us'. The world, contrary to popular opinion, is not made up of 'real sinners' – the mass murderers and the like – and 'ordinary decent people' who, needless to say, have never done anything 'really bad'! *All* have sinned and come short of the glory of God. And to approach God with your lips, while your heart is far from him, is a most basic manifestation of contempt for God. It is not to be trivialized. It is the radical contradiction of the first commandment: 'You shall have no other gods before me' (Exodus 20:3), and the 'first and greatest commandment' of the Lord Jesus Christ: 'Love the Lord your

God with all your heart and with all your soul and with all your mind' (Matthew 22:37,38).

The 'cows of Bashan' did not love their neighbours as themselves (Matthew 22:39). But, before that, they did not love the Lord their God with heart, soul and mind. Their sin challenges our consciences, therefore, in a most relevant and searching manner. Let us notice how they behaved and apply the lessons to ourselves and to our churches.

1.   They attended church services from time to time: **'Go to Bethel and sin; go to Gilgal and sin yet more.'** Bethel and Gilgal were the sites of Israel's golden calf worship. They perpetuated the sin of Jeroboam I (1 Kings 12:26-33). They worshipped God in their terms, rather than in his. He said, 'in Jerusalem', they said, 'No!' He said, 'no idols'; they made golden calves. The new theology ruled; the Bible was set aside; man was the measure of things – even of the things of God; the worship of God became will-worship – the glorification of the imaginations of men over against the claims of an inerrant Word from God himself. The Bethels and Gilgals of our time abound in the shells of Christian churches gone to seed in the Bible-unbelieving, doctrineless and Christless theologies of the twentieth century. 'Go to Bethel and sin!' stands as the Lord's rebuke to the empty religion of our day!

2.   They observed all sorts of ritual. The Lord's response is scathing. Suppose they brought their **'sacrifices every morning'**, their **'tithes every three days'**?[1] Suppose they **'burn[ed] leavened bread as a thank-offering'**? Now, the sacrifices were to be offered only *once* (1 Samuel 1:3,7,21). The tithes were only to be given every *year* (Leviticus 27:30). Leavened bread may, from one point of view, be an improvement on unleavened bread, but it is the latter that God had commanded to be used exclusively in the burnt-offerings (Leviticus 2:11; 7:12,13). But what would they care about what God's Word says? They would point out that they were doing

---

[1]The Hebrew is *yamim,* which means every triad of *days,* not years. See C.F.Keil and F.Delitzsch, *Commentary on the Old Testament,* Vol.X, p.271, for a thorough discussion of the exegesis of this passage.

more than even God had asked, would they not? So why should
God complain? And the prophet's point is that though they
were to follow such a rigorous course of ritual observances, it
would avail them nothing. If they thought the frequency of
their worship, or the value of their tithes, was impressive to
God, then let them reflect on what God actually required of
them – not a lot of outward and even expensive show, but the
'sacrifices of a broken spirit and a contrite heart' (Psalm 51:17,
AV).

3.   They **'brag[ged] about their free-will offerings'.** It was
their pleasure to do their 'acts of righteousness' before men, to
be seen by them' (Matthew 6:1). Our Lord said that our giving
should be 'in secret' (Matthew 6:4). This has not deterred
churches in our own day from publishing the givings of the
members, presumably with the approval of enough of them to
override the scriptural objections of those who take the Lord's
words seriously! There are churches that raise money by
promising each donor that a plaque bearing his or her name
will be displayed on that part of the building paid for by the
donation. There are many ways of bringing self-glorification
into Christian piety. No doubt it stimulates giving to offer to
put the donors' names on the bricks their money buys. But, like
the giving of the 'cows of Bashan', it all adds up to the rejection
of the Lord's way of faithfulness (Matthew 6:1-18). 'Secret'
allows no leeway, either in the attitude of the heart or the
action of the hand. Indeed, it is the very readiness to be unseen
and unsung that is the touchstone of the life of faith in the heart
when it comes to Christian good works. Pride always craves
recognition. Publicity is its life-blood. But Christian humility
confides secretly in the Lord and awaits his reward in his time
(1 Peter 5:6). Grace in the heart is what was missing in the
ladies of Samaria. All that they did that was outwardly good
was to serve the spirit of self-righteousness. And so the prophet
says, **'"Boast about them, you Israelites, for this is what
you love to do" declares the sovereign Lord'** (4:5).

What is especially tragic in this situation is that Israel had
been given the Word of God and had seen the mighty acts of
God in her national history and experience. How sad that such
blessings should have been thrown away! It was such waste to

turn away from the gift of life. I vividly recall an incident in my childhood that has remained as an illustration of this fatal tendency in human nature. We were privileged to have a swimming teacher who was both a lovely lady and a mistress of her craft. She was a gold medallist in the 1924 Olympic Games and a world record holder in her own event. We eight-year-olds were awed by her and we felt very safe in her hands – except one class-mate. His fear of the water overcame him and he refused to take the lesson. And he walked away, affirming – in that way that children often do – that he would rather risk drowning in the future than go into that pool today! The world would rather drown in its own cesspool of self-righteousness and self-sufficiency than follow God's way. That is why the 'cows of Bashan' ended up as they did. The Lord takes no pleasure whatsoever in this. He does not delight in human self-destruction or in his own righteous judgements upon reprobate humanity. He does not send prophets like Amos to depress us and cast us down into despair with their pronouncements of wrath to come. God's purpose is primarily a purpose of grace. He wishes to shake us by the blasts of his Word, so that we might recognize him for who he is – the God who maintains love to thousands, but who does not leave the guilty unpunished (Exodus 34:7).

We are invited, in that paradox of all prophecy of judgement, to choose life rather than death. Jesus lamented over a Jerusalem that would shortly be destroyed: 'O Jerusalem, Jerusalem, you who kill the prophets and stone those sent to you, how often I have longed to gather your children together, as a hen gathers her chicks under her wings, but you were not willing. Look, your house is left to you desolate. For I tell you, you will not see me again until you say, "Blessed is he who comes in the name of the Lord"' (Matthew 23:37-39).

Come, in the name of the Lord.

Questions for study and discussion

1. Compare the wives in Amos 4:1 with 1 Peter 3:1-6. What was the duty of the wives in Israel? To encourage their husbands? Apply this to the relative roles of husband and wife today in our consumer society.

2. It is unlikely that these women were *directly* involved in the various oppressions which their husbands committed against the poor. Their sin was to incite their husbands to greater excesses, e.g. 'Bring us some drinks!'

    a. Discuss the relationship between heart and hand with respect to the guilt of sin. (See Proverbs 4:23; 16:23; 21:4; Jeremiah 17:9; Matthew 5:28; Luke 12:34; Hebrews 10:22.)

    b. What is *complicity in error?* Discuss the sin of Achan and the complicity of others in his sin (Joshua 7). Can a nation be guilty of the wicked policies of her leaders? Why is *dissent* such an important right? Why must Christians bear *testimony* to Christ in community life?

3. Was God fully justified in his judgements? (4:2,3) What does this say to our situation? To God's people? To our nation?

4. Discuss the problems with Israel's religion and apply it to our own day:

    a. *Church attendance.* Why was it a sin to go to Bethel and Gilgal? (See 1 Kings 12:26-33.) What does this mean for your attendance at worship? What kind of worship should it be? (Deuteronomy 12:32; Matthew 28:19,20.)

    b. *Ritualism.* Why is outward ritual so attractive? What does God think of the multiplication of observances? (See Psalm 51.)

    c. *Showy do-goodism.* Read Matthew 6:1-18 and contrast with Amos 4:4,5. Why are we to be secretive in our giving? Why is humility essential? (1 Peter 5:6.)

5. Are the accounts of God's judgements meant to depress us? Read Matthew 23:37-39 and discuss the notion that the gospel of Christ is always the silver lining on the clouds of prophetic wrath. What response is God looking for?

6.
Prepare to meet your God!

Please read Amos 4:6-13

'There are none so blind as those that do not want to see.' This proverbial wisdom is surely descriptive of sinners in general and, in the context of this passage, the Israelites in particular. Israel had been reminded of her sins – moral, social, political and religious. She had been informed, in no uncertain terms, of God's future visitations of judgement. The writing was on the wall. Israel had been weighed in the balance and been found wanting.

Now, lest there be any objection that God had somehow failed to give them fair warning, Amos points them to that most basic awareness of every human heart, namely, the awareness that we are the creatures of a creator God and that we live in a world that he has made. It is as if God says to us, 'Even if you have shut your ears and minds to my Word and to the prophets, you can never escape the clear teaching of creation and providence, which, in its simple, intuitive and non-verbal way, constantly reminds you of the God you have so wronged and reveals to you his wrath from heaven.' As the apostle Paul later wrote, 'The wrath of God is being revealed from heaven against all the godlessness and wickedness of men who suppress the truth by their wickedness, since what may be known about God is plain to them, because God has made it plain to them. For since the creation of the world God's invisible qualities – his eternal power and divine nature – have been clearly seen, being understood from what has been made, so that men are without excuse' (Romans 1:18-20). This is the point of contact that God's message has with any and all men, irrespective of their spiritual darkness. All men are therefore without excuse! They know it too! And that is why they have

67

bad consciences and very often an ill humour when confronted
by the gospel of Christ.

Amos is speaking, however, to God's backslidden covenant
people rather than to the heathen. The fact that they – God's
people – remain unmoved by his message all the more justifies
the righteous indignation of the Most High and serves to
colour with dark majesty the foreboding words he soon utters:
'Prepare to meet your God, O Israel' (Amos 4:12). Before these
unutterably solemn words the whole human race stands with
dread expectation. When, in Matthew Arnold's poem 'Sohrab
and Rustum', the Persians beheld the battle array of the
Tartars by the river Oxus, 'The pale Persians held their breath
with fear.' Destruction by a superior foe stared them in the
face. Men, as if already dead, clutched sword and spear with
the *rigor mortis* of terrified enervation. Yet Israel, in the face of
divine wrath and a judgement extending to the second death of
a lost eternity, goes careless and unprepared into the presence
of God! This our passage explains in graphic simplicity.

Clear warning (4:6-11)

Five general judgements are mentioned.
1.   **'I gave you empty stomachs in every city'** (4:6). There
had been famine in the land from time to time.
2.   **'I also withheld rain from you'** (4:7,8). Drought had
variously affected different areas – an experience common to
most countries throughout history.
3.   **'I struck your gardens and vineyards ... with blight
and mildew** (4:9). They were also afflicted with plagues of
locusts.
4.   **'I sent plagues among you'** (4:10). Disease and war had
ravaged the population. God did this, he said, **'as I did to
Egypt,'** – an unmistakable indication that it was the finger of
God pointing to their sins and the need for their repentance
(Exodus 8:19).
5.   **'I overthrew some of you as I overthrew Sodom and
Gomorrah'** (4:11). Here the reference is to earthquakes
destroying towns and villages. These too are pointers to God's

wrath with their backslidings, for Sodom would have been spared for the sake of as few as ten righteous men, had they resided there (Genesis 18:32).

Evidently these events – what we call 'natural disasters' – had occurred relatively recently, at least in terms of the national consciousness of such things. They were, from God's point of view, episodic warnings set against a background of national prosperity and spiritual and moral decline.

Such phenomena occur in every day and age. In our days of mass communication we are virtually inundated with news reports on all these subjects. We might even be inclined to forgive the cynic who says, 'No wonder the Israelites did not listen to Amos. After all, these are not unusual, abnormal or miraculous events. So, is it not merely a matter of opinion that such things should be seen as God's judgements? We can explain them in naturalistic terms, so who needs to invoke an angry Divinity?' How, then, are such objections to be answered?

One answer would be to say that these particular events recorded in Amos 4 were *direct* warnings from God. That is to say, that while they were natural disasters, they were accompanied by some indication that God was speaking in them. This, however, does not do justice to Romans 1:18-23 and emasculates the Bible's doctrine of general revelation, which is that everything in the natural world is revelational of God's eternal power and divine nature.

A more satisfactory approach is surely to recognize that we are face to face with the way we are to understand natural phenomena – and, indeed, history itself. Thinking about such matters as famine, weather, disease and war, Herman Veldkamp commented, 'This revelation also affects our own point of view. What God says here is not the kind of thing we normally say to one another, nor is it the kind of thing we read in the newspapers. I am the One! Some people regard it as old-fashioned to speak of God's judgements in such a context. Others explain the problem of our time on the basis of earthly factors, such as economic conditions, international tensions, and mistakes made by government. And there is indeed a place for this kind of explanation – provided we do not forget that

God is at work in and behind all of this. I am the One!'[1]

What does this imply for our practical attitude to the providential course of our lives? Surely this: that *all the problems in the world are essentially spiritual in nature*. This is not at all to remove the element of the technical from any problem. For example, better management and more efficient farming has improved the food situation in India. But will there ever be the blessing that God would give as long as a false religion dominates and allows 'sacred' cows to enjoy, unhindered, a large portion of the resources needed for human beings? The same can be said with respect to the condition of our own country. Economics and education can neither define nor solve adequately the obvious social disintegration and moral anarchy around us. The Word of God, however, interprets this situation infallibly and provides the solution in the person of Jesus Christ. God's warnings, in the very fabric of day-to-day experience of natural phenomena and the changing conditions of our society, are as plain as a pikestaff. And it is equally obvious, from the reading of the Bible, that were men and women to obey God through faith in the Lord Jesus Christ as a personal Saviour and sovereign Lord, the face of human society would be transformed. Genuine blessing, spiritual and temporal, would pour forth beyond measure, as it has done in the spiritual revivals of the not-so-distant past. Amos's fundamental point is that faith, repentance and a return to holy obedience are called for from sinners, if there is to be real blessing – indeed, if there is to be escape from God's just wrath! **'"Yet you have not returned to me," declares the Lord,'** is the lamentable refrain (4:6,8-11).

Meeting God (4:12)

Five times, and with increasing intensity, God declared his judgements as Israel had *already* experienced them. Five times he records their lack of positive response. In the last of these cycles of warning (4:11) there is even a highlighting of the

---

[1] H. Veldkamp, *The Farmer from Tekoa*, p.128.

grace that God had shown on at least one occasion in their recent history: **'You were like a burning stick snatched from the fire'** (Isaiah 7:4; Zechariah 3:2). They had been delivered from calamity at the last minute, yet they could not see God's grace in it and still did not repent!

What is there for the Lord to do with them? 'All day long' God held out his hands to 'an obstinate people' and, therefore, he will 'measure into their laps the full payment for their former deeds' (Isaiah 65:2,7).

'Therefore this is what I will do to you, Israel' (4:12a). The word 'therefore' is emphatic. The cup of wickedness is full and the reckoning has come. The antecedent verses of the chapter tell the story, as we have seen. The root of the problem is spiritual and the most obvious manifestation of this is the religion they practised (4:4,5). They liked to think they were right with God, whatever they did. Like the Pharisees in Jesus' day, they had 'a fine way of setting aside the commands of God in order to observe [their] own traditions' (Mark 7:9). These 'traditions' – which were, in fact, human inventions that cut across what God wanted of them – in turn became a defence mechanism against the real spirituality, grace and glory of God's plan for the lives of men and women. They were God's covenant people; they professed to be his children; yet they were not satisfied with his Word, the whole Word and nothing but the Word.

The contemporary application is unmistakable, as Herman Veldkamp has so searchingly pointed out in his inimitable fashion: 'We love to make up our own religion. The tendency to seek a religion outside and above the church is assuming many and new forms. Many people are ready to tear down the church walls, arguing that they are of no further use. The air inside those walls is much too stuffy . . . There's no warmth and love in the church. Furthermore, what difference does the church make? On judgement day we will be asked not to what church we belonged, but whether we loved Jesus.

'The fool who utters these sentiments usurps the judgement seat of Christ and takes it upon himself to decide "what we will be asked". This fool goes overboard with the "love of Christ" and denies Him His claim to "obedience", thereby committing a sin worse than revolution. This fool tries to kick down the

church doors that Christ Himself promised to defend against
the gates of hell. This fool despises the church that Christ
Himself loved and founded and bought with His blood. Do you
suppose the King of Kings sitting at God's right hand will
remain unmoved by this mutiny in the name of piety and
freedom . . . ?'[2]

Let us examine our lives. Do we add to God's Word? Do we
take away from its teaching? Do we love some little traditions
so much that they assume greater importance than Scripture
itself in determining how we shall behave or with whom we
shall share fellowship? Are we honestly, sincerely, diligently
and faithfully following the Lord Jesus Christ?

**'And because I will do this to you, prepare to meet your
God, O Israel'** (4:12b). The 'this' is never defined. The
judgement is open-ended, except that it involves meeting God.
'Prepare to meet your God' is a slogan beloved of cartoonists
with a penchant for ridiculing the Christian message, but there
are few more solemn words. Men who laugh at God must be
terribly sure that they will never meet him, though on what
basis they should be so confident is a mystery. Israel must meet
him. All men must meet him (Romans 14:10; 2 Corinthians
5:10). Israel had time to prepare and we know how well that
time was used. You have time to prepare, but how will it be
with you? When the books are opened and the full story told,
will you be found to have come to Christ, resting entirely on his
full atonement for sin and pleading his mercy and merits for
your salvation? Or will you go blithely on, careless of your soul
and your eternal destiny, perhaps trusting in the rags of your
own self-invented righteousness to pull you through somehow?
Time is short! Now is the day of salvation!

The majestic God (4:13)

There was a time when the Royal Navy only had to sail a ship
near some potential trouble-spot to nip the problem in the bud.

---

[2] H. Veldkamp, *The Farmer from Tekoa*, pp.134-135.

As the Falklands War of 1982 showed, it takes more than one vessel on station to deter and defeat a potential aggressor. The 'gunboat up the river' policy rested on the idea that a *token* of the available power should be sufficient to cow the 'natives' and obviate any necessity to use that power. The great powers use 'sabre-rattling' to effect policy.

The living God is doing something similar in Amos 4:13. Without giving an exhaustive account of his attributes and his power, he reveals himself in terms of representative characteristics. He, in a sense, 'rattles' his sabre. 'Would you meddle with me? Then consider who I am! I am the Lord God Almighty! Do not under-estimate me!'

God challenges them: 'Look at the mountains and ask who formed them. Make weather forecasts, but remember who creates the wind. You can think, but who knows your thoughts? You can light the night with artificial light, but can you darken the day? Who treads the high places of the earth? Who is in control of the elements? Who causes the rain to fall? Who is working out all of history according to an eternal plan and purpose? The Lord God Almighty is his name.

'This is what the Lord says: See, I am setting before you the way of life and the way of death . . . ' (Jeremiah 21:8).

Questions for study and discussion

1. How should we interpret phenomena such as the events of 4:6-11? As messages from God – to be heeded for our blessing – or just as 'the luck of the draw'? Discuss the idea that all the world's problems are *essentially* spiritual. How do we put that together with the technical or scientific approach to solving difficulties?
2. If Israel had listened to Moses and the prophets, would God's wrath have been revealed from heaven against them?
3. Discuss the repeatedly used phrase, '. . . yet you have not returned to me'. Israel was like 'a burning stick snatched

from the fire' (4:11). What does this tell us about God's attitude to Israel?

4. They are to *prepare* to meet God. God is speaking to the church here. What is he looking for? (See Matthew 18:1-6; John 3:1-8.)

5. God gives a glimpse of himself in 4:13. Why? What does he mean to convey to the minds of his hearers? What should our response be? What is your response – in your heart – today?

7.
Seek me and live!

Please read Amos 5:1-17

Inscribed in stone over a gateway at King's College, Aberdeen, are the words of the university's motto: *Initium sapientiae timor Domini*. One wonders how many of the students that pass by know that it is a quotation from the Bible and that it expresses the commitment of the medieval founders of the college to the proposition that true education centres in the knowledge of God! 'The fear of the Lord is the beginning of wisdom' is a truth repeated frequently in the Word of God (Psalm 111:10; Proverbs 1:7; 9:10; Job 28:28).

What is significant about this idea, in relation to Amos's ministry of judgement, is the thought that it is in the *fear* of God that wisdom finds its beginning. There is surely an analogy with the preaching and the hearing of the gospel – or, to be more explicit, with the ministry of the whole Word of God, both law and gospel, judgement to come and redemption to be received. The Word of God calls us to believe in the Lord Jesus Christ, the only begotten Son of God, that we should not *perish*, but have everlasting *life*.

There is, of course, fear . . . and fear! There is the sheer terror of the fear of God's wrath and there is the grace of the reverent fear of the Lord, which is related to the 'spirit of sonship' that belongs to every true child of God (Romans 8:15). Whether the fear of God is a craven, unbelieving terror, or a reverent, believing awe of a personal Father-God, it is still a *fear*, and it is a fear that is rooted in the character of God as the one who cannot look upon sin. As such, that fear – in a manner appropriate to the psycho-spiritual condition of believers and unbelievers respectively – is designed to concentrate minds on the holiness of God and what his will is for our lives. To the non-Christian conscience, this fear of God is resisted and suppressed, unless God the Holy Spirit sovereignly and powerfully draws that sinner to himself by spiritual rebirth and conversion to Jesus Christ. To the Christian, the fear of God is nothing less than the treasuring of the knowledge of God in Christ, in his heart and in the joy of an everlasting salvation.

When Amos declares the displeasure of God with the sheer wickedness of Israel, he no doubt means to shake his hearers in their shoes. He means to put the fear of God in them. And yet there is throughout the passage more than a hint of the possibility of coming to the Lord afresh, in faith and repentance, and so experiencing that perfect love that casts out fear – that perfect love which is, paradoxically, rooted in the 'fear of the Lord'.

This paradox leaps at us again and again from our passage of contrasts. The phrase, **'Hear this word . . .'** introduces a most trenchant pronouncement of divine judgement (compare 3:1; 4:1). The message itself consists of two parts. The first of these is a lament for fallen Israel (5:2,3). The second (5:4-17) is a fast-moving, rather unstructured but impassioned plea for the doomed people to **'seek the Lord and live'** – even at the eleventh hour of their national existence.

The theme is most beautifully expressed in the incomparable language of the Authorized Version rendering of Amos 5:8: 'Seek him that maketh the seven stars and Orion, and turneth the shadow of death into the morning, and maketh the day dark with night: that calleth for the waters of the sea, and poureth them out upon the face of the earth: The Lord is his name.' You will have noticed, if you are using a modern translation, that the AV has added the word 'seek' – a word not in the original Hebrew. This, however, does accurately convey the gist of the verse and is to be preferred to the NIV rendering, which, rather curiously, puts the whole text in parenthesis. Israel, like the psalmist, is walking through the valley of the shadow of death (Psalm 23:4) but, unlike him, is not trusting in the Lord for deliverance. Two strands intertwine throughout: the inevitability of the destruction of wicked Israel, on the one hand, and the urgency of the call to repentance and salvation from the wrath to come, on the other hand.

It's your funeral! (5:1-3)

One of the most striking images of my youth was the scene in the film version of Edgar Allen Poe's *The Premature Burial,* in which Ray Milland – actually alive, but believed to be dead – has to watch through the glass window of his coffin (only in the films) as the words of the committal are read and earth is thrown into the grave. Long before 'horror stories' the same dramatic device was used by Amos! When Amos declares his lament for fallen Israel it is, as E.B. Pusey put it, 'as if a living man in the midst of his pride and luxury and buoyant recklessness could see his own funeral procession and hear, as it were, over himself, "Earth to earth, ashes to ashes, dust to dust."' Amos reads Israel's obituary over her living corpse! He says to the professing church (for Israel was a branch of the church of the Old Testament), 'Look into your coffin and see your true spiritual state – soon to be your physical state also! Continue as you are, Israel, but realize that it is your funeral!'

'Fallen is Virgin Israel . . . (5:2). Israel is called a 'virgin', not because she is pure and unsullied, but because she has been independent as a nation up till now. In this sense she is a 'virgin'. This will end. She will fall **'never to rise again'** and with **'no one to lift her up'.** So will perish one of the 'denominations' of the Old Testament church! We do not need to look far for a word of warning to the modern church. In his letter to the church at Sardis, the apostle John left no room for doubt as to the mind of God in this matter – and this, of course, applies to the church in every age and not just in first-century Asia Minor. He wrote, 'I know your deeds; you have a reputation of being alive, but you are dead. Wake up! Strengthen what remains, and is about to die, for I have not found your deeds complete in the sight of my God. Remember, therefore, what you have received and heard; obey it and repent. But if you do not wake up, I will come like a thief, and you will not know at what time I will come to you' (Revelation 3:1-3). Church history is littered with the memorials of congregations and whole denominations that once flourished and are now gone for ever, together with the distinctive doctrines they believed were the unchangeable Word of God and for which they felt they had to contend even to the division of the Body of Christ! Why did they disappear? No doubt many reasons could be suggested: 'The young people didn't stay in the church.' 'It's a "day of small things".' 'We couldn't afford to repair the buildings.' What it all boils down to, in the end, is the withdrawal of God's blessing as *per* the letters to the seven churches of Revelation 2:1-3:22. 'He who has an ear, let him hear what the Spirit says to the churches' (Revelation 3:22).

What about churches that are still apparently alive? The message is for the living, not for the dead and gone! Israel was outwardly quite prosperous. Many churches today are similarly thriving. There is a great deal of activity, a well-developed programme, a wide range of organizations catering for every age group in church and community and perhaps even thronged services on the Lord's Day. Israel may have been *dead*, from God's point of view, but you would not have said so had you seen the statistics on church attendance and giving. We must therefore, look at the deeper things, 'The more important matters of the law – justice, mercy and faithfulness' (Matthew 23:23). Speaking of the superficial trappings of much of modern church life, Herman Veldkamp asks, very pointedly, 'Where, amid all the loud applause, are we to find the shy blossoming of life? Where, amid all the noise and cheering, is the living testimony of Jesus Christ? Where is the tender life of prayer, and where are the ripening fruits of the inner life of faith?'[1]

Israel's prosperity, military prowess and ersatz spirituality could not save her. The statistics of defeat are as conclusive as they are grim:

> 'The city that marches out a thousand strong for Israel
>   will have only a hundred left;
> the town that marches out a hundred strong
>   will have only ten left' (5:3).

Apostasy, however magnificent its panoply and power, will perish for the lack of a real soul. 'Where there is no vision [i.e.

---

[1] H. Veldkamp, *The Farmer from Tekoa*, p.153.

revelation – the Word of God *believed*] the people perish'
(Proverbs 29:18, AV).

Seek the Lord and live! (5:4-17)

God once again challenges the church. This almost symphonic
passage moves rapidly from one vital thought to another as it
heaps up reasons for Israel's extinction and urgently calls for
repentance. All of the problems have previously received the
prophet's attention. These are (a)   false religion (5:5,6; cf.
3:14; 4:4,5), and (b) social injustice (5:7,10-13; cf. 2:6-8; 3:15;
4:1). Overarching these are the claims of God, in all their
ineffable majesty (5:8,9,14,15). Three important consider-
ations are apparent, each of which affords further insight into
our contemporary experience.
1.   *The mirage of man-made religion* (5:4-6). Israel had no
shortage of religion. There were sacrifices and tithes and
offerings. No doubt they took comfort in God's covenant
promises and in their own religious observances. The fact that
they worshipped in Gilgal and Bethel – and, it seems, even in
Beersheba, away to the south of Jerusalem – when God had
commanded them to worship him in Jerusalem, apparently did
not trouble them. After all, they were 'sincere' – or, at least,
they did go to church sometimes. Like the nominal 'Christians'
of today, whose discernible devotion to the Lord extends no
farther than sporadic attendance at Sunday services and a £1
coin in the plate, the Israelites had adopted an easy religion
that provided enough, to their way of thinking, to insure
themselves against any potential wrath of God in the next life,
without interfering very much with what they wanted to do
with their lives in this world. They could feel good about
themselves and their relationship to God at the cost of a little
outward religious observance that would never challenge their
hearts and minds with the radical claims which, in actual fact,
are made by the Word of God. They were ready to accept the
assurances of God's covenant without taking any of its real
stipulations seriously. Such people live in the mirage of what
we might call 'covenant smugness'. They are the people who

are so blind to their own unbelief and folly that they will protest, even as they are thrust into hell, 'Lord, Lord, did we not prophesy in your name, and in your name drive out demons and perform many miracles?' What is the Lord's answer? 'I never knew you. Away from me, you evildoers!' (Matthew 7:22,23).

2.   *The certainty of God's judgement on unrepented sin* (5:8-13,16,17). As Amos preaches, one has a sense of his increasing doubt that Israel will be saved. The last two verses (5:16,17) surpass even his earlier lament for fallen Israel (5:2,3) in their portrayal of the wrath to come: **'There will be wailing in all the vineyards, for I will pass through your midst.'** We are reminded of the Passover in Egypt, when the Lord passed *over* the children of Israel in the process of destroying the first-born of Egypt. Here the Lord passes *through* Israel, for it is Israel who must feel the cutting edge of offended justice. In Egypt, the blood of the sacrifice was smeared on the lintels of Israel's doors – a symbol of efficacious atonement made for the sins of the people. In Samaria, the blood of the sacrifices offered on the false altars of Bethel and Gilgal is a stench in God's nostrils. No efficacious blood is, as it were, on the lintels of Samaria – that is to say, faith that looks to the sovereign grace of God in salvation is not to be found in the hearts of the people. Sin is unrepented. Indeed, what God called sin has been redefined as permissible in the thinking of Israel. Amos, speaking under the direct inspiration of God, senses the inevitability of the woes he prophesies. He knows that he has a ministry of judgement rather than one of revival. Yet it is clear that he does not despair of there being any blessing at all. It is equally clear that God takes no pleasure in the destruction of Israel, wicked as they undoubtedly are.

3.   *The free offer of the gospel* (5:4,6,14,15). The full message of the New Testament in Jesus' blood – the fully sufficient, once-for-all, sacrificial, atoning death of Christ in behalf of lost sinners – has yet to be revealed when Amos is preaching. But within the light of the types and shadows of the Old Testament, Amos preaches the gospel. **'Seek the Lord and live'** (5:6) could not be a more luminous invitation for someone in need of God's saving grace. It is an invitation to

life. All else is death, including the soothing ministrations of
the liberal clergy at Bethel! There is no middle way. Agnostics
are not going to be saved by their doubts, nor hypocrites by
their show of piety. The Lord must be your Saviour and Lord
or you are lost . . . and lost in hell for all eternity! The intensity
of the call to salvation deepens as the prophet speaks: **'Seek me
and live . . . Seek the Lord and live . . . Seek good, not evil,
that you may live'** (5:4,6,14). He is the personal God who
says, 'Seek *me*.' He is the covenant God who reveals himself as
Yahweh – the *Lord* – and whose love has been upon his
believing people from the beginning. He is the holy God who
cannot look upon sin and so calls men to seek '*good*, not evil'.

When we draw these three strands together – false religion,
certain judgement upon unrepented sin and the gospel offer of
salvation – we can see some of the tensions and difficulties
attending the ministry of God's servants in this world. The
ministry of Amos is particularly instructive. If anyone felt the
resistance of his hearers to his message, it must have been
Amos. Certainly, if he had tied his encouragement and
persistence in the ministry to *statistical* success, he might soon
have joined the ranks of 'burnt out' ministers, who can take the
frustration of an apparent lack of positive response no longer!
But Amos knew that his would be a difficult task. He knew that
it was largely a ministry of judgement, although not without its
offer of grace and promise of victory. In this respect, his
expectations would have been quite different from those of the
apostles and, indeed, the preachers of the Christian gospel
right down to the present day. Amos looked forward to the
Messiah, in terms of the Old Testament forms and shadows,
while the New Testament church, in the fulness of the
revelation of the crucified and risen Saviour and the
outpouring of the Holy Spirit since Pentecost, proclaims the
accomplished victory of Christ and the imminence of his
return. Nevertheless, there are lessons to be learned from Amos
for our ministry today.

1.   There will always be a mixed reception for the preaching
of God's Word. The world is not dying to hear the message of
the gospel; it is dying in its sins. The world is predisposed to
resist the gospel, because the gospel calls for the greatest

change people can experience in their lives – from darkness to light, even the light of Christ. The gospel is the 'aroma of Christ among those who are being saved and those who are perishing. To the one we are the smell of death; to the other the fragrance of life' (2 Corinthians 2:15,16). Some will grow, but others will go!

2.   Faithfulness in the ministry is in the proclamation of the Word, prayerfully and in the demonstration of the Spirit's power (1 Corinthians 2:4). Paul planted, Apollos watered, 'but God made it grow' (1 Corinthians 3:6). Success – in the number of those who hear the message and come to follow Christ – is actually the work of God, who draws people to Christ by his Holy Spirit (John 6:44; cf. John 3:6-8,16). This, in turn, is rooted in the eternal purpose of God: 'that God's purpose in election might stand' (Romans 9:10-24). Faithfulness rests in the absolute sovereignty of God, believing that he will perfectly accomplish his will.

3.   The ultimate triumph of God's purpose of redemption is assured. For Amos, the advent of the Lord Jesus Christ was eight centuries into the future, but he looked, by faith, to his coming and knew that the Lord would accomplish his purpose. We live between the two advents of Christ: after the cross and the resurrection, but before the Parousia – the second coming of Christ, at the end of the age. The ministry of the message of redemption is, therefore, as the apostle Paul asserted, a 'triumphal procession in Christ'. The gospel of saving grace is the means by which 'the fragrance of the knowledge of him' (i.e. Christ) is extended to the human race until the very end of the present age (2 Corinthians 2:14). Christ has overcome the world (John 16:33). Christ is the 'head over everything for the church' (Ephesians 1:22). Christ is coming again to gather all his people to himself (1 Thessalonians 4:16,17).

Amos preached the truth from God. He would have rejoiced with the angels in heaven had they repented and returned to the Lord. But Amos's sense of God's glory and his purpose of grace was not diminished by Israel's collective insistence on perishing in their sins. Amos knew that there would be a remnant according to the election of God's grace (Romans 11:5). He knew that the Messiah would come and the true

Israel of God be restored and revived (Amos 9:11-15). He knew that for all who would follow the Lord in time to come, the **'shadow of death'** would be truly and eternally **'turned into morning'** (5:8). And so it is to this day! Jesus Christ is the promised Saviour! Jesus Christ died to save sinners, such as we are! The Word of God says, 'Now is the time of God's favour, now is the day of salvation' (2 Corinthians 6:2); 'Salvation is found in no one else, for there is no other name under heaven given to men by which we must be saved' (Acts 4:12). **'Seek the Lord and live!'**

Questions for study and discussion

1. Amos delivers a 'lament' – a funeral oration – over Israel (5:1-3). What is his purpose? Look up Luke 12:4,5 and Proverbs 9:10 and discuss the use of fear in spiritual things. When will fear cease to be used by the Lord in the Christian's experience? (1 Corinthians 13:10; 1 John 4:18.)
2. Israel represents the apostasy of the church of the Old Testament era. What can the New Testament church learn from this? Read Revelation 3:1-6. Why was God saying that the congregation in Sardis might close its doors? And how might it avoid this end? Compare with the other churches in Revelation 2:1-3:22. Why are churches closing today – and others thriving?
3. What is God's attitude to unrepented sin? (5:8-13,16,17) How does this affect the Christian life? (Psalm 66:18; Matthew 5:23,24; 1 Corinthians 11:27-34.)
4. What does it mean to 'seek the Lord and live'? (5:4,6,14,15) Why must sin and judgement be preached in connection with the gospel of saving grace in Jesus Christ? Get a concordance and look up the New Testament references using the word 'repentance' (Greek, *'metanoia'*). (See especially Acts 2:38; 3:19; 17:30; 20:21; Luke 13:3-5; 2 Peter 3:9.)

5.   Amos did not see mass conversions or the salvation of
the nation of Israel through his preaching. Was he a
'success' or a 'failure'? What is our criterion of success in
the service of God? (Romans 9:10-24; 1 Corinthians 3:6,7;
2 Corinthians 2:15,16.) Are you a 'fair weather' Christian?
What was the apostle Paul like? (1 Corinthians 9:26; 15:32; 1
Timothy 6:12; 2 Timothy 4:7.)

8.
The Day of the Lord

Please read Amos 5:18-27

The story is told of two men who were discussing the whys and wherefores of the biblical 'millennium' mentioned in Revelation 20:4. Which of the three classic interpretations of this period was correct? Was it *pre*millennialism, *post*millennialism or *a*millennialism?[1] 'Oh,' said the one man, 'I have the solution to the problem. I call it "*pan*millennialism".' His companion was puzzled. 'What is "panmillennialism"?' he asked. 'It means,' came the reply, 'that everything will pan out all right in the end!'

The serious point here is that millions of people think about death and eternity in this way. They think it will work out all right, for them, in the end. Even atheists think this way, because their belief that they cease to exist at the moment of death is really a kind of faith and hope that there is no life after death and no judgement in the hands of an infinite-personal God. Annihilation may not appeal to everyone, but it has to be more attractive than eternity in hell! That is things 'panning out' all right, from the atheistic point of view! Of course, those that profess to be Christians and the devotees of a number of other religions that anticipate a life after death are looking for something positive and preferably paradisiacal. The Christian hope centres on a reconciled and redeemed state, in fellowship

---

[1] *Pre* millennialsm holds that Christ will return *before* a literal thousand-year millennium. *Post*millennialism believes that Christ will return *after* a millennial 'golden age'. *A*millennialism regards the present age, between the two advents of Christ, as an inaugurated or realized millennium.

with God, through the perfect atonement made by the Lord
Jesus Christ in his sufferings and death. This hope belongs,
properly, to those who, in repentance towards God and faith in
the Lord Jesus Christ, have come to know Christ as their
Saviour and Lord. Yet it is incontrovertible that many who
know nothing of personal faith in Christ and have no more
than an outward perfunctory religion, devoid of what Scripture
defines as true discipleship – the love of Christ in the heart and
in diligent obedience to the teaching of God's inspired Word –
are, nevertheless, quite confident that they will go to heaven
when they die. Their ministers have told them that there is no
hell and God means to save everyone in the end. Perhaps they
have been told that when they die they will go into the presence
of God and that experience will so transform them as to fit
them for heaven. No wonder that universalism is so popular
with so many people!

Israel, like so many in our day, was happy with her religion,
in spite of the fact that she knew very well that the plain
unvarnished Word of God presented an entirely different
picture of what it meant to serve the living God. The same
is true today among the clerics and people of the most
prominent churches in this country. They deny that the Bible
is the inspired, infallible and inerrant Word of God; they
reject the cardinal teachings of the Bible, as 'myths' unworthy
of modern scientific man; they regard Christ as no more
than a good teacher – if you can discover the 'historical Jesus'
in the morass of apostolic fables called the New Testament;
and they see God as no more than a construct of the human
mind, or an existential encounter with the 'wholly other',
whatever that may be. Yet, somehow, they cling to a hope of
heaven and are convinced that, if there is such a place and
anyone is going there, they will be admitted in due course. The
Israelites were comfortable with their highly favourable
religious system. They were not pleased with prophets who
came along and reminded them of their sins and the obvious
incongruity of their lives when measured against what the
Word of God actually said. They were glad to retain the
privileged covenant relationship with God which he had
revealed to their forefathers. This, they imagined, made them

right with God – or as right as they needed to be for all practical purposes. They engaged in religious observances, even as an integral part of national life. They 'professed faith' *and* 'went to church' *and* gave 'tithes and offerings' and, as Amos 5:18 reveals, even looked forward to 'the day of the Lord'. But all the while, they cheated the poor and lived lives of unrestrained materialism and debauchery.

To this monstrous presumption God's servant brings more than a whiff of God's grape-shot. Israel *longs* for the Day of the Lord? Then let them understand what that day will mean for their present and eternal destiny!

A lion, a bear and a snake (5:18-20)

'Woe to you who long for the day of the Lord!' (5:18) Israel looks forward to a special day – 'the day of the Lord.' This is the earliest use of the expression 'day of the Lord' in Scripture.[2] This day is spoken of in the prophets and in the New Testament. In the New Testament it refers to the second coming of Christ, that is, the Day of Judgement (Matthew 25:31-46; Acts 17:31; Romans 2:5-10; 1 Thessalonians 5:2; 2 Thessalonians 1:7-10; 2 Peter 3:10-13). The prophets prepare the way for this with a broader concept of the Day of the Lord that includes both the final day *and* the events of God's providence throughout history. This day is simply the visitation of divine justice. In Amos 5:18 Israel is in view (as also Isaiah 2:12-21; Joel 1:15; 2:1,11 and Zechariah 14:1), while in other passages it is other nations that are involved (Isaiah 13:6,9; Obadiah 15). All these will come to a final consummation in the coming of the Lord (Joel 2:28-32). What this boils down to is that, when Israel longed for the Day of the Lord, they were looking forward to the judgements of God upon their enemies in the short term and to their final vindication by God in the long term. It was evidently something they talked about, and with

---

[2] See the article 'Day of the Lord' in *The New Bible Dictionary*, London, IVP, (1962), pp.296-7.

great self-assurance and joyous anticipation. Israel was a bit like a lapsed church member who, when challenged about his three years non-attendance by the newly inducted pastor, retorted indignantly that he would look forward to the Day of Judgement, when he would see the pastor 'get it in the neck' for his 'judgemental attitude' in suggesting he was 'in sin' by not attending public worship!

Israel and modern mankind need to understand what God is really doing in history, that is, what the Day of the Lord is all about. This day is actually a present reality in this sin-sick world. It is like a volcano that is building up to a great final eruption. Down the centuries there are minor eruptions and rumblings – the tokens of the power within that is yet to be released. So the day breaks into the experience of men and nations from time to time, but awaits the literal last great day for the consummation of all things.

We are, therefore, never justified in putting off the matter of our relationship to the Lord. We do this with examinations. We put off studying until the last minute. But how good are we 'on the day'? The practical import of the Bible's teaching is on the 'now' of Christ's invitation to come to him as the only Saviour. Now is the day of salvation!

Surely it is amazing that Israel saw no danger for herself in the coming Day of the Lord. They sincerely believed that God was on their side. Perhaps the very material prosperity of their nation convinced them that this was the case. It did not seem to occur to them that their practical disregard for God's will, as revealed in his Word, could incur the displeasure of God. Happy sinners are always practical atheists. Whatever they say about God, they live their lives as if he were not there and had not the slightest interest in taking his own Word seriously! As long as they are not being actually struck down by thunderbolts, they feel God must be reasonably pleased with them. Besides, even disasters can be blamed on other people's wickedness. Whether men regard their prosperity as a mark of God's favour or their poverty as a qualification for divine compensation, they remain blind to the 'finger of God' and harden their hearts against the real lessons of experience. Amos once again spells out the danger in no uncertain terms:

'That day will be darkness, not light' (5:18c). He illustrates this with a story. They will be like the man who meets a lion and escapes only to meet a bear. He eludes the bear and, doubtless exhausted but exultantly relieved, he slams the door shut on the animal, leans on the wall – and is fatally bitten by a snake secreted in a crack! Just when he thought he was safe! Israel had been delivered from many disasters – perhaps famine, or economic ruin, or foreign enemies. They are now prospering. They are safe. But the truth is that the enemy is within. The enemy is the God in whom they so presumptuously trust – the God they have remade in their own image, the God they have replaced with a convenient deity that winks at their sin and massages their ego! The real enemy is themselves, of course. It is their 'sinful mind' that is 'hostile to God' (Romans 8:7). They have alienated God and must face the consequences. What Joel said about the great day was that 'Everyone who calls on the name of the Lord will be saved' (Joel 2:32). What do the lion, the bear and the snake teach us? 'Unless you repent, you too will all perish' (Luke 13:5). So said the Lord Jesus Christ. Only the truth of God will be upheld on the Day of the Lord. Only those washed in the blood of the Lamb will hear the words: 'Come, you who are blessed by my Father; take your inheritance, the kingdom prepared for you since the creation of the world' (Matthew 25:34).

The 'church' God hates (5:21-23)

We have already seen what God thinks of 'churchianity'.[3] The parallels with modern church life are all here.

'I hate, I despise your religious feasts' (5:21). What should have been the very gate of heaven, and a wonderful means of grace to changed hearts and discipled lives, had become the very means by which they hardened their unchanged hearts and papered over their sins with a fancy and

---

[3] See chapter 5 and the comments on Amos 4:4,5.

expensive covering of empty ritualism. What offends God is the brazen way men justify themselves and take to themselves all the comfort and assurance of the covenant faithfulness of God, while setting aside the law of God.

'Even though you bring me ... offerings ... I will not accept them' (5:22). God's interest is not in the perfunctory observance of the correct *form*, but in the proper *attitude of heart* as the motive for outward obedience. He is offended by people who draw near to him with their lips, while their hearts are far from him (Matthew 15:8,9). The Old Testament, contrary to popular misconception, is full of this truth. Examples abound from Genesis to Malachi (Genesis 4:5-7; 1 Samuel 4:3-11; Psalm 51:16,17; Isaiah 1:10-15; Malachi 1:10,14; 2:1-3,13,14). One of the most startling examples of this is in 1 Samuel 15. King Saul had been commanded by God to destroy the Amalekites – lock, stock and barrel. Saul, however, modified this commission and kept the best sheep and cattle from the plunder and, not least, spared Agag, the Amalekite king. When challenged by the prophet Samuel, Saul weakly protested that he had obeyed God and had only kept back the best animals for sacrifice to the Lord at Gilgal. To this came Samuel's memorable reply:

> 'Does the Lord delight in burnt offerings and sacrifices
>   as much as in obedience to the voice of the Lord?
> To obey is better than sacrifice,
>   and to heed is better than the fat of rams.
> For rebellion is like the sin of divination,
>   and arrogance like the evil of idolatry'
>   (1 Samuel 15:22,23).

Saul was, thereby, rejected by the Lord as the King of Israel.

'Away with the noise of your songs!' (5:23) expresses the same theme, but with reference to their music and praise in worship. It is mere *'noise'*. It may entertain them and make them feel good, but it annoys God. No doubt they invented new forms of praise to 'improve' the worship of Israel, just as they had invented golden calves and extra sacrifices as 'aids to devotion'. The analogies with the so-called 'gospel concert' scene today are unmistakable.[4] Praise has become entertainment and totally obscured in the haze of false joy lies the forgotten content of the revealed will of God and the true meaning and enjoyment of spiritual union and communion with the God and Father of our Lord Jesus Christ.

The heart and soul of the problem is *formalism*, that is, 'having a *form* of godliness but denying its power' (2 Timothy 3:5) and trusting in that mere outward observance to win God's approval. 'For not all who are descended from Israel are Israel,' wrote the apostle Paul (Romans 9:6). A true Jew, the apostle tells us, is the man who 'is one inwardly; and circumcision is circumcision of the heart, by the Spirit, not by the written code. Such a man's praise is not from men, but from God' (Romans 2:29). So it is, of course, with the true Christian. Being a Christian means much more than having some 'profession' in words only or in merely outward actions. 'What a godly profession had Judas!' wrote Matthew Mead, 'He followed Christ, left all for Christ; he preached the gospel of Christ, he cast out devils in the name of Christ, he ate and drank at the table of Christ;and yet Judas was but a hypocrite.'[5]

The only alternative: justice and righteousness (5:24-27)

There is a glorious nugget of grace in the middle of all the woe: **'But let justice roll on like a river and righteousness like a never-failing stream.'** There is another way. In contrast with the institutionalized hypocrisy of their culture, there could be the justice and righteousness prescribed by

---

[4] J. Blanchard, *Pop goes the Gospel* (Evangelical Press, 1983) provides a most thought-provoking analysis of the gospel entertainment phenomenon. See especially pages 75-140.

[5] Matthew Mead, *The Almost Christian Discovered* (Philadelphia: Presbyterian Board of Publication, orig. publ. 1661) pp.48,49.

the Lord. Away with your feasts, your offerings and your
songs! Live forth the justice and righteousness of the law
of God! Live in covenant faithfulness to the pattern of holiness
revealed to you in the Scriptures. This should pour like a river
from the hearts of the Lord's people! It should be a never-
failing stream in their body-life as his holy nation! To
emphasize the point and the issue before them, the Lord
mentions two things.

First of all, he asks them if they brought him **'sacrifices and
offerings'** during their wanderings in the wilderness (5:25).
No doubt they would answer in the affirmative. Yet it seems
unlikely that that is the answer that God is looking for. The
point is, surely, that sacrifices were not the main thing that
they brought to the Lord. Rather it was *obedience*, in response to
the law given at Sinai, that was the central aim of their lives
and, indeed, the goal of such sacrifices as were commanded
under the law. Though a generation perished in the wilderness
because of their unfaithfulness, those that entered the
promised land did so as a spiritually alive and blessed
covenant nation, walking in holiness before the Lord.

Secondly, and in stark contrast, the present state of their
hearts is opened to public view: **'You have lifted up the
shrine of your king, the pedestal of your idols, the star of
your god – which you made for yourselves'** (7:26). There
are difficulties with the translation of this verse. The references
are probably to pagan deities incorporated in the worship of
Bethel and Gilgal. The translators of the Septuagint, the Greek
Old Testament, thought the 'shrine' was that of Moloch and
the 'idols' and 'god' the deities of the Assyrians. The point is
that Israel was virtually pagan, under its extensive vocabulary
of 'God talk' from the Scriptures. In their hearts, they are light-
years away from the living God! Therefore, they will be exiled
'beyond Damascus', that is, in the land of the very people
whose gods they now so assiduously court!

Can it be said that justice rolls like a river and righteousness
in a never-failing stream in the modern church? Or in your
daily life? 'The evidence of true religion,' writes J.A. Motyer,
'is that it touches all life with the holiness of obedience to His
Word and command. He will not endlessly live with the stench

of false religion in His nostrils and its noise in His sears.'[6]
May the Lord Jesus Christ live richly in your heart by his Spirit
and may his righteousness pour forth like a never-failing
stream in your life by saving faith and his unquenchable love!

Questions for study and discussion

1. What is the meaning and significance of the Day of the
    Lord for the history of the world and the experience of the
    church in the world? (See Hebrews 3:7,13,15.)
2. Discuss the 'snake in the wall' story (5:19).What does this
    say to the spiritual life of the church today? Who will be
    saved in the great day? (Joel 2:32; Luke 13:5; Matthew
    25:34.)
3. What was the problem with Israel's religion? (Read 1
    Samuel 15 and compare it with 2 Timothy 3:5; Romans
    2:29; 9:6.) What did Jesus mean in Matthew 5:20? Discuss
    the case of Judas Iscariot.
4. Discuss 5:24 in the light of John 7:38. Contrast this call to
    godliness with the condition of Israel. Why is 'heart
    religion' so vital? (Jeremiah 17:9,10; Psalm 14:1; 51:10;
    66:18; 119:10,11; Proverbs 3:3; 14:30; Matthew 5:8;
    12:34,35; 22:37; Luke 12:34; Galatians 4:6; Hebrews
    10:22; 1 Peter 1:22.)
5. What is your prophetic responsibility to those members of
    your church fellowship whose idea of membership seems
    to have no place for (a) regular attendance at the stated
    services of worship, (b) corporate prayer, (c) eagerness for
    fellowship with God's people and (d) practical
    discipleship – in the use of time, gifts and personal
    conversation and ethics?
    (You will find J.C. Ryle's *The True Christian* (Evangelical
    Press: 1978) of inestimable value for your ministry to
    others and not least for your own personal discipleship to
    Christ.)

---

[6] J.A. Motyer, *The Day of the Lion*, (IVP; 1974), p.137.

9.
A false sense of security

Please read Amos 6:1-14

In the closing scene of the film of *The Bridge over the River Kwai*, just about everybody in the picture dies in an orgy of destruction, in which a British raiding party destroys a Japanese train on the Japanese bridge newly completed with British POW blood and sweat. James Donald, who pays the POW camp medic, surveys the devastation and utters the last words of the film: 'Madness! . . . Madness! . . . Madness!'

It is a parable of the despair with which modern man views the human condition. Man is in the grip of a self-destructive madness, of which war is its most lunatic expression.

We all feel that sense of helpless frustration when we see someone hurtling, unawares, to a doom of their own creation. It is axiomatic that such destruction is not foreseen at the time it is being courted. Heroism in war is probably the exception that proves the rule. The people in the Titanic (the ship that someone said even God couldn't sink) were having a great time until the ship ran into an iceberg. It is the long view, the perspective of experience and history, that reveals the endemic folly of human confidence. 'It will never happen to me' passes into history as false prophecy. So much optimism is simply false. So much security is an illusion – a mere construct of a human mind that cannot face the real facts.

The Bible is a book about security, because it is the Word of *God* – the Rock of salvation and strong tower (Psalm 89:26; Proverbs 18:10) – and it is a word to *lost mankind* about the only security there is in the universe, namely, belonging to God as the sheep of his pasture (Psalm 23; John 10:1-30). When Scripture speaks about false security, it does so in order to offer true security in its place. Jesus Christ came to seek and to save the lost. The Christian is one whose life is hidden with Christ in God (Colossians 3:3). Christ is his guarantor (Hebrews 7:22).

Amos comes to people who think they are safe enough but, in fact, are living in a dream. They have everything they need in the way of security in this life and a most suitable religion to look after the next! They are a complacent people. To this, Amos comes with what are probably the most familiar words of his entire prophecy: **'Woe to them that are at ease in Zion and trust in the mountain of Samaria'** (6:1, AV). Then in the accents of irony and satire, the prophet takes apart the Israelite 'castles in the air!' The passage unfolds in three distinct phases. First of all, in 6:1-3, God challenges their complacency. Secondly, in 6:4-7, he takes away the first pillar of their security – their wealth. Finally, in 6:8-14, he removes the second pillar of their confidence – their power. This is the last of the series of five 'judgements' recorded in Amos 3:1 – 6:14.

Complacency challenged (6:1-3)

God speaks first to the **'notable men of the foremost nation'** (6:1). The nation referred to here is the whole of God's covenant people – both Israel and Judah. This is evident from the references to Zion as well as Samaria. Both are *'at ease'*. Both are guilty. Both are to be rebuked.

They feel secure. They are complacent. But what are the facts? Amos calls them to account: firstly, with an ironic illustration of the emptiness of their position (6:2) and secondly, with a chilling and scathing description of their true plight (6:3).

'Go to Calneh and look at it . . .' They are to consider Calneh, Hamath and Gath. **'Are you better than those kingdoms? Was their land larger than yours?'** The answer is 'Yes, Israel is better' and 'No, their land is not larger.' These are only city-states on the border of Israel. The point is that Israel is just a big fish in a small puddle. If these little countries, which are militarily insignificant, are the reason for Israel feeling so big and powerful, then Israel must think again. We are always inclined to magnify our self-images by measuring them against the lowest possible denominator. We are like the schoolboy who told everyone that he was good at 'mathematics' on the basis of a 96% result in an arithmetic test! When the poor lad had to face some algebra – real mathematics – he was notably unsuccessful. The Dervishes believed that they would defeat the British invasion of the Sudan in 1898, because the mullahs had assured them that bullets would not kill 'the faithful'. General Kitchener's Maxim guns put paid to that tragic confidence at the Battle of Omdurman! Israel must know that Assyria was no Calneh! 'Look up and see the real enemy,' Amos might have said, 'and then tell me how secure you really are!'

'You put off the evil day and bring near a reign of terror' (6:3). False confidence, in other words, is counter-productive. It actually brings the reckoning closer. Why? Because the climate bred by such delusion can only foster the conditions which will encourage a powerful enemy to feel that he can strike sooner than he thought he might. At a deeper level still is the consideration that God's anger is incurred by that same climate of wickedness and unreality with respect to spiritual things.

The classic case is perhaps that of the rich fool, in the parable recorded in Luke 12:13-21. Confronted with better crops than anticipated, this man decided to build bigger barns for his equivalent of the EEC grain mountain: 'This is what I'll do. I will tear down my barns and build bigger ones, and there I will store all my grain and my goods. And I'll say to myself, "You have plenty of good things laid up for many years. Take life easy; eat, drink and be merry."' 'But God said to him, "You fool! This very night your life will be demanded from you. Then who will get what you have prepared for yourself?"' 'This is how it will be with anyone who stores up things for himself but is not rich towards God.' The man was a fool because he thought 'things' afforded security, when in fact, the only security is in being 'rich towards God', that is having a personal saving faith in God through the Lord Jesus Christ.

The end of wealth (6:4-7)

Two great pillars of Israel's false sense of security are now kicked away by the prophet. The first is their wealth, which manifests itself in debauchery. The second, to which we shall return later, is their power, expressed in injustice and militarism.

'You lie on beds inlaid with ivory and lounge on your couches' (6:4-6). This passage does not teach asceticism – the doctrine that physical comforts are wrong in themselves and that it is therefore the duty of Christians to subsist, as opposed to seeking a comfortable style of life. The Word of God promises more than the barest necessities to believers and it is simply impossible to explain away such promises of prosperity as referring exclusively to the inner spiritual cultivation of the soul. (Compare Proverbs 13:11; Psalm 112:3; Ephesians 4:28 with Deuteronomy 8:11-20; Proverbs 18:11; James 5:1-6). It is *excess* that is the concern of the prophet Amos.

1. There is an obsession with luxury and fine feasting (6:4). Some years ago, during one of these episodic outbursts of awareness in the West that there really are millions of starving, dying people in other parts of the world, a cartoon appeared which portrayed a well-dressed and portly gentleman, sitting at a table laden with food and wolfing down as much as he could. A small boy was standing beside him and was holding out a collecting can, labelled 'Freedom from Hunger'. Says the man to the boy, without going into his pocket for a contribution, 'Sure, I believe in freedom from hunger, son!'

2. They were inordinately concerned with entertainment (6:5). **'You strum away on your harps like David and improvise on musical instruments.'** Whether this was, as has been suggested by some commentators, the profanation the worship of God by the introduction of unwarranted music is really impossible to determine.[1] It is by no means impossible that something akin to Belshazzar's infamous feast took place at Bethel. Suffice it to say that the place of entertainment was

---

[1] No doubt Amos is referring to David's introduction of musical instruments into the temple worship (1 Chronicles 23:5; 2 Chronicles 29:25,26). This is

such that it had become a major means of escaping the claims
of reality.

3.   The same can be said for over-indulgence with wine
(6:6a): **'You drink wine by the bowlful . . . ',** thereby
perverting a gift of God.

4.   Then there is tremendous personal vanity (6:6b): **'. . . and
use the finest lotions,'** and, finally,

5.   There is a hard-hearted disregard for the very fabric of the
nation and, in particular, the suffering of the poor and
oppressed, who bear the real cost of all the 'good times' of the
'notable men' and the 'cows of Bashan'. They **'do not grieve
over the ruin of Joseph'.** They are centred in self.

'**Therefore you will be among the first to go into exile;
your feasting and lounging will end'** (6:7). The leaders will
be seen to lose their pirated privileges by those whom they
oppressed, as they head the dreary columns stumbling to the
east. Wealth – one of their real 'gods' – has failed them. The
party is over.

The end of power (6:8-14)

God declares that he abhors **'the pride of Jacob'** and detests
'his fortresses' (6:8). So collapses the vaunted power of Israel.
What follows in its train includes all the ravages of pestilence
and war. Cities will fall to the enemy (6:8); houses, great and
small, will be destroyed (6:11); and the people will die in such
numbers that whole families will be annihilated and distant
relatives will have to dispose of the bodies (6:9,10). The
corpses would be cremated – a practice prescribed in God's
law as a penalty for certain cases of gross wickedness (Leviticus
20:14; 21:9) – thereby signifying the retributive justice of God,

---

not a criticism of David but an ironic barb directed at the 'entertainment'
clique, who perhaps liked to use David as an excuse for their unholy
innovations. There is surely a clear application to the churchmen of today
who have turned their churches into concert halls and substituted chamber
music for the worship of God's people and to the 'gospel entertainers' who
similarly baptize, with a presumption of biblical authority, forms of music
inconsistent with the true spirit of praise.

for the honourable disposal of the dead was exclusively by burial.

Amos emphasizes the truth that it is foolish to trust in military power (Psalm 20:7), by means of some rather cryptic remarks: **'Do horses run on the rocky crags? Does one plough there with oxen?'** The answer is, of course, a resounding 'No!' That would be irrational. No one in his right mind would dream of doing such things. Well, says Amos, you have shown about as much intelligence in two things that you have done.

1.   You abused your power to oppress the people, by turning **'justice into poison and the fruit of righteousness into bitterness'** (6:12).

2.   You rejoiced in your military prowess and boasted about the bogus achievements of conquering Lo-Debar (literally, and significantly, a place called 'not anything!') and Karnaim. These insignificant towns had been wrested from the Aramaeans in an earlier campaign.

For this, the Lord will stir up some real power that will sweep through Israel from Lebo Hamath in the north to the shore of the Dead Sea in the south (6:14). Before the strength of Assyria, the Israelite armies will melt away!

We are reminded in all this of the words of 1 Samuel 4:21,22: 'She named the boy Ichabod, saying, "The glory has departed from Israel" – because of the capture of the ark of God and the deaths of her father-in-law and her husband. She said, "The glory has departed from Israel, for the ark of God has been captured."' The end of Israel teaches us about the seriousness of backsliding and apostasy from God. Taken together with the teaching of the New Testament, there is much to apply to the life of the church today, as we have been seeing in these studies. Overarching these warnings, however, stands the greater truth that the covenant love of God was not extinguished for mankind – nor will it ever be extinguished – by the covenant-breaking even of those who were his people under the external administration of the covenant. God's purpose to save a people stands throughout all generations and, in the fulness of the time, he sent his only begotten Son, the Lord Jesus Christ, 'born of a woman, born under law, to redeem those under the law, that we might receive the full rights as sons' (Galatians 4:4,5). 'Ichabod' was written over one 'Israel', but Christ is the name upon the true 'Israel of God' (Galatians 6:16). His shed blood is upon the lintels of believers' hearts. Indeed, they are washed clean from sin by his death in their place. Jesus Christ is the Saviour! There is life in him for all who will believe! This, ultimately, is the meaning of the prophecy of Amos.

Questions for study and discussion

1. What is wrong with Israel's sense of security? Can you think of any modern equivalents to Calneh, Hamath and Gath? What is God's security for men and women? (2 Corinthians 12:9. See also Psalm 23; John 10.)
2. Why does 'putting off the evil day' bring near a reign of terror? (6:3) See Luke 12:13-21 and discuss how this applies to personal attitudes to security and also to the policies of the state.
3. What do the excesses of Israel's leaders mean for the way a Christian lives and particularly his attitude to material comforts and the 'consumer society'? (See Deuteronomy 8:11-20; Ephesians 4:8; 2 Corinthians 8:13-15; 9:6-9.)
4. What happened to Israel? (6:9,10,14)
5. Remembering that Israel was not merely a nation, but part of the church of the Old Testament, how can we learn lessons from her experience for the life and witness of our own church fellowships? How are we to deal with backsliding in our personal lives and in the fellowship? (Matthew 18:15-20; Acts 15:1-35; 1 Corinthians 5:1-13; 6:1-8; 2 Corinthians 6:14-18; 1 Timothy 3:1-11; Titus 2:1; Hebrews 13:7,17; James 4:7-10; James 5:13; 1 Peter 5:1-6; 1 John 5:16.)

10.
Opposition to God's Word

Please read Amos 7:1-17

The five predictions of judgement upon Israel recorded in Amos 3:1-6:14 are now followed up by a series of five visions which illustrate Israel's predicament. This section comprises Amos 7:1-9:10 and it should be read in its entirety before proceeding to the specific studies in the next three chapters. These visions serve to heighten the drama and intensify the urgency of the prophet's message. They also prepare the way for the final section of the prophecy, which speaks of the promise of revival under the Messiah who is to come (Amos 9:11-15). This will be the subject of the last chapter of this book.

From the human standpoint, few ministries would seem as discouraging as that of Amos. The message he was given to preach is, in itself, almost enough to crush a man's soul. This is true, in a sense, of the very task of preaching God's Word in a fallen world where the will of God inevitably cuts across just about everything that sinners hold dear. We must preach about sin, about God's law and about death and eternity. But, unlike Amos, we have the full gospel of Jesus Christ – Christ revealed in his finished work and risen in his triumph over sin and death – and not merely the promise of Christ's coming. Furthermore, we have the Holy Spirit, poured out upon the church since Pentecost, to be our Comforter who leads us into all truth (John 14:26; Acts 2:1-4). And this has meant, for nearly two thousand years, the conversion to Christ of millions of people across the world, a work of grace that shows no sign of abating in our own generation, as the church of Jesus Christ in the Third World and behind the Iron Curtain experiences unprecedented growth and spiritual refreshment. Amos, in contrast, saw virtually no positive response. He laboured on, preaching judgement upon judgement, yet pointing to the way of salvation here and there, but it is as if no one is moved, no one really cares!

The present chapter, however, does bring a decided response to God's Word. Amaziah, a priest from Bethel, rises up in indignation against Amos and attempts to silence the prophet (7:10-13). It appears, from the flow of the text, that the priest heard Amos speaking of the content of the visions God had shown him and this establishment cleric was so infuriated that he felt compelled to enlist the forces of the state to stop the prophet's mouth and censor the truth that God had given to him. He seems to have broken into Amos's discourse and sought to silence him on the spot. We shall see, in due course, how Amos deals with this interruption. But first we must see what precipitated Amaziah's furious outburst.

The locusts and the drought (7:1-6)

The five visions, the first two of which are here revealed, teach basically the same truth. The main difference between them is that there is a steady progression in severity with each new vision. The first two visions are taken together because, in both cases, God relents in response to the prophet's prayer and does not bring about the disasters he had prepared.

'He was preparing swarms of locusts' (7:1-3). These swarms arose between the first crop – the mowing taken by the king for his horses (1 Samuel 8:12-15; 1 Kings 18:5,6) – and the second crop, which was essential for the people to feed their cattle and thus, ultimately, themselves. This calls forth the earnest prayer of the prophet. He intercedes for Israel: **'How can Jacob survive? He is so small!'** God hears and relents. The disaster previewed in the vision is averted. 'The prayer of a righteous man is powerful and effective' (James 5:16).

'The Sovereign Lord was calling for judgement by fire' (7:4-6). Here the very source of water for the land, 'the great deep,' would be dried up. The land would be scorched, no doubt as so much of the Sahel region in Africa has been devastated in recent years. Again, the prophet prayed for this not to happen and God heard his prayer. **'"This will not happen either," the Sovereign Lord said'** (7:6).

There are striking similarities between these two cases and they teach us truths of the utmost relevance to our present experience.

1.   These are so-called 'natural' disasters. In fact they are the movements of God's providence – the judgements of God in history. This again raises the question as to how we are to interpret natural calamities.[1] The assessment of naturalism – the doctrine that 'this world' is all there is and the various factors operative within it are exhaustively intelligible in terms of their intrinsic properties – is that such things 'happen' as part of the natural 'system', albeit apparently by 'chance'. That is to say, there is no supernatural upholding and direction of the natural world and it is basically 'the luck of the draw', or sometimes the folly of man, that natural disasters strike as they do. The Bible, in contrast, sees all events as falling within the eternal plan and purpose of God. It may be that man's folly creates environmental disasters. It may be that otherwise unpredictable turns of events, such as a volcanic eruption or a typhoon, wreak havoc apparently 'by chance'. It is, nevertheless, the 'finger of God'. As such, it ought to call forth holy and awesome thoughts of God. We ought to be humbled. We ought to fall to our knees. We ought to pray for mercy. We ought to reflect upon our relationship to the Lord and, indeed, that of others so afflicted. And this ought to bring us face to face with the waywardness of our own lives and the causes of God's displeasure with us! The idea that a *loving* God would never permit such events to occur, far less actually bring them about, has wide currency today, even among professing Christians. This does no justice, either to the Lord God himself, or to the sinfulness of human sin. Were the critics of the Bible's clear teaching in this matter to assess their own depravity of heart and mind against the holiness of God, they would count it *grace*, as the psalmist did, to be called to account

---

[1] See pp. 44-46

by affliction (Psalm 119:67). Paul expressed the same thought when he declared that the afflictions he was experiencing were achieving an eternal glory that far outweighed all his troubles (2 Corinthians 4:17).

2.   The basic Christian response, apart from confessing that the Lord is just in all his ways, must be to pray, as did Amos. He asks God to forgive and to save Israel. It is no slip of the tongue that he asks for pardon before he asks for the removal of the locusts. He realizes that the cause of the problem must be dealt with first. One fears that much of the prayer offered by people who have 'found religion' in hard times is *first* prayer for removal of the discomfort of the trouble, and *second*, a hurried 'Forgive us our sins for Jesus' sake, Amen.' The spiritual man discerns the real problem and gets to the heart of the matter. Herman Veldkamp aptly sums this up, when he writes, 'What filled him [Amos] with fear was not the swarm of insects but the spiritual decay that had long ago robbed Israel of its purity. What Amos feared was sin! Behind all the problems and plagues of our time is the guilt of the world and the church.'[2]

So Amos calls on his covenant God: 'Sovereign Lord, forgive!' (7:2) He uses the covenant name Yahweh – rendered LORD in the NIV.   He pleads for covenant mercy . . . for free grace. 'How can Jacob survive? He is so small!' We are always small in our own sight when we truly pray to the Lord. True prayer is very humbling, because it is the exact opposite of pride and self-sufficiency. It is the cry of a refugee for help. It is an appeal to grace from a position of helplessness.

3.   Amos, the preacher of judgement, is a man of compassion and prayer. Others write him off as a doom-monger with a hard heart, who thrills to fire and brimstone messages and visions of the lost in hell. This passage shows such charges to be an utter travesty of the truth. Amos is seen to be what every preacher of the Word of God must be – one who is faithful to the ministry that God has given to him and who, like the apostle Paul, does not hesitate to warn his hearers 'night and day with tears' (Acts 20:31). The pastor worth his salt agonizes

---

[2] H. Veldkamp. *The Farmer from Tekoa*, p.201.

over his people for he keeps watch over them as one who must
'give an account' (Hebrews 13:17). It is love for God and love
for souls that motivates Amos, and must be the motive of every
Christian's witness for Christ today.

Measuring up (7:7-9)

The third vision – the vision of the plumb-line – is not one of
devastation, but it is rather more foreboding than the first two.
The Lord is here seen as a kind of building inspector. He is
standing beside a wall – which represents Israel – and is about
to measure it with a plumb-line. The plumb-line is only a
measuring instrument. It detects whether the wall is sagging or
is true to the vertical. It is able to tell the inspector whether the
wall is sound or whether it will have to be pulled down as a
danger to public safety. The plumb-line is, in the vision, a
pointer to the most awful pronouncement yet, for God, having
applied the test, declares of Israel, **'I will spare them no
longer'** (7:8). He then goes on to detail the destruction of the
religious and civil establishments of Israel: **'The high places
of Isaac will be destroyed and the sanctuaries of Israel
will be ruined; with my sword I will rise against the house
of Jeroboam'** (7:9). The vision itself may not be one of
devastation but it surely presages devastation on a grand scale.
The plumb-line – the test – makes failure official. Israel has
not measured up. The prophet has no prayer. And God does
not relent.

The modern church cannot evade the thrust of this
prophecy. There are at least two areas of immediate relevance.
1.   First is the matter of *testing*, which is, after all, the main
theme of the vision of the plumb-line. The Lord is checking the
soundness of the building. He checks the walls of the church, of
the family and of the individual. His purpose is positive. He is
not a mere 'fault-finder'. The very testing involves the content
of the Scriptures and the searching probes of the Holy Spirit
into the conscience. The gospel itself is the laser of God's
holiness, exposing the wound and bringing the healing at
one and the same time. Christ is like the 'refiner's fire'

(Malachi 3:2). He calls even as he tests – but test he does – and there is a day to come for every human being when the results will be manifest.

2.   Secondly, we must note that the idea of the church as a spiritual *building* is essential to the understanding of the vision. It is the church that is under scrutiny. It must also be recognized that, against the measure of God's perfect law, she always fails. We are reminded, however, that the New Testament tells us that Christ is the corner-stone and is building his church into a temple of the Holy Spirit, out of stones that once were dead and are now made alive by grace through faith (1 Peter 2:4-10). Veldkamp opens this up for us in the most striking and beautiful manner: 'The church will be preserved only because it knows and believes that its King was measured with a plumb-line, that He was torn down like a badly sagging wall, that he was battered and earned the name *Man of sorrows*. Although He was perfect, He was made to pay for what's wrong with our walls.'[3]

Of the glory of the church, the prophet Isaiah wrote,
   'I will build you with stones of turquoise,
      your foundations with sapphires.
   I will make your battlements of rubies,
      your gates of sparkling jewels,
      and all your walls of precious stones'
                                    (Isaiah 54:11,12).

Christ has done this by bearing away our sins in his own body on the cross. In Christ the plumb-line is the righteousness that can, that must be ours. In Christ the plumb-line hangs flush against the converted sinner, for his sins are covered by Christ's substitutionary atoning death and the Saviour's righteousness accounted to the believer as his own. In Christ the wall does not sag but stands vertical and sound, rebuilt by the hand of the Lord and pointed by the Word and Spirit!

   Here is the good news behind the dark rumblings of the

---

[3] H. Veldkamp. *The Farmer from Tekoa*, p.208.

vision! There is a way of life! Christ is that way! 'Believe in the Lord Jesus, and you will be saved . . .' (Acts 16:31).

Here comes trouble! (7:10-17)

It is obvious that if God has to send a missionary prophet from Judah to get his message to the people of Israel, the preachers in Israel must be in a bad spiritual state. The establishment preachers of Israel are, needless to say, dedicated to the *status quo* in their country rather than the radical righteousness of Yahweh. It is no surprise, then, when opposition arises from the ranks of the ecclesiastical establishment. Enter Amaziah, the priest of Bethel! (7:10)

Amaziah's opposition to God's message is typical of overt attempts to censor the truth. There is, of course, the covert approach, of which many of God's servants are only too painfully aware: the cold silence and the placid correctness that masks a seething discontent with the message; the 'helpful suggestions' that 'warmer' (and shorter) sermons would stimulate greater commitment from the people. Then a pressure group arises and it is said that 'Some of us are concerned that we are not growing as we might because of an imbalance in the messages,' that is, too much 'sin' and not enough 'love'. And then come the Amaziahs and open warfare!

Notice what Amaziah does.

1. *He calls on the 'powers that be'*, in this case, the king, because he is the subject of the prophet's declaration (7:10a). In the context of an evangelical preacher in a mainline modernistic church, it might be the bishop, or the local presbytery or association, depending on the form of church government. In Communist countries – or Muslim, for that matter – the state is invoked, perhaps even, in the former case, with the connivance of the 'official' or 'registered' clergy. In any event, the 'big guns' are called upon.

2. *He puts the worst possible construction on the good man's words* (7:10b-11). There is a **'conspiracy'** and **'the land cannot bear his words',** that is, he is a menace to social stability and public welfare. Amaziah presents it all as a personal threat to

Jeroboam and the nation. The loving entreaties, the appeals to return to the Lord and the prayers for mercy are perversely overlooked. The priest has very cleverly begun to shift the ground from principles to personalities. And it is almost always the same in church controversies today. The man is tackled rather than the ball. Show that he has personality problems or merely a 'personality conflict' and the embarrassing necessity of dealing with the actual merits of the case – whether he is preaching the truth of God, or not – can be avoided and the way paved for his replacement by a more acceptable preacher!

3. *He exploits nationalistic prejudice:* **'Get out, you seer! Go back to the land of Judah'** (7:12). This is always a powerful card to play, when a pretext is needed for removing someone who happens to have a different background. 'He's a foreigner, you see. He doesn't understand us. He never quite fitted in. He would be better going back where he belongs!' Again, principles of truth can be circumvented by an appeal to base sentiments.

4. *He charges God's servant with mere professionalism* (7:12d). Amos was not the last minister to be accused of being 'on the make'! Nothing will destroy a man's standing with the public more quickly than the charge that he is 'in it for the money'! The truth was that it was the Amaziahs of the world who were the time-serving professionals who gave the people what they wanted and troubled no one but those sound in the faith over their doctrine or their ethics.

5. *He implied a certain illegitimacy in Amos's preaching at Bethel* (7:13). Bethel is **'the king's sanctuary and the temple of the kingdom'.** When all else fails, use 'procedure'. Thus God can be silenced on a technicality! That is to say, any excuse will do to suppress the Word of God. It is not that Amaziah does not think of himself as a man of liberal views. Amos can preach – in Judah; he can earn his living by preaching – in Judah; but he has no business disturbing Israel!

How does Amos respond? He defends his commission from God and he goes on practising it faithfully!

For the record, he denies Amaziah's accusations of being a professional prophet. He was a farmer and well able to support himself. He preached to Israel only because God had expressly commissioned him to do so! (7:14,15) There is a wealth of instruction in the way God's servants defend themselves before their detractors. Whether it is Amos, Peter, Stephen, Paul or the Lord Jesus Christ himself, the defence offered is succinct, humble and Spirit-given (Acts 4:8-12; 5:29-32; 7:1-53; 22:2-21; 23:1-7; 24:10-21; 26:2-29; Galatians 1:11-2:21; Matthew 12:25-37; 21:23-27; 26:62-64).

Furthermore, Amos refuses to be silenced. He specifically prophesies Amaziah's end and that of his family and his nation. The spiritual rot that engendered the opposition to God's Word receives its answer in the most rigorous affirmation of that Word (7:16,17). Censorship does not alter the facts. God has spoken! Christ is risen! Where will you stand at his appearing?

Questions for study and discussion

1. Compare and contrast the first two visions. What do they teach us? How are we to think of natural disasters? (Psalm 119:67; 2 Corinthians 4:17.)
2. Why does Amos pray for forgiveness? (7:2) Why not just pray for relief from the trouble? Can verses 2 and 5 teach us about the way we are to pray?
3. What is the main point of the vision of the plumb-line? Compare Daniel 5:27 (the testing of unbelief) with Romans 14:18; 1 Corinthians 11:19; James 1:12.
4. Discuss how the idea of a building is used in relation to the church. (See Matthew 16:18; Ephesians 2:19-22; 1 Peter 2:4-10.)
5. In what ways did Amaziah (and modern detractors of the faithful ministry of the Word) express opposition to God's messenger? Trace the sequence in Amos 7:10-13.
6. How did Amos respond? (7:14-17) How ought we to respond to such criticism? (1 Corinthians 4:3-5.)

11.
A famine of the Word of God

Please read Amos 8:1-14

The fourth vision must have baffled Amos at first. It was a basket of ripe fruit – a symbol of all that is wholesome and healthful, one might have thought. In the United States of America, such a basket is the standard gift for people recovering from illness in hospital. It looks good, it tastes good, it is good, and it conveys good wishes for health and strength. It is good for you. With respect to Israel, however, the meaning is quite different, as becomes apparent when God interprets the vision for the prophet.

A new train of thought is unfolded, which casts a fresh light on God's controversy with Israel. Three points are made about Israel's condition and future prospects: Israel has only an appearance of health, masking the fact that she is ripe for judgement (8:1-3); Israel's oppression of the poor will result in present joy being turned into mourning (8:4-10); and the land will be overtaken by a famine – a famine of the Word of God (8:11-14).

Ripe for judgement (8:1-3)

In the autumn it is customary for Christians to thank God for the farmers' harvest. The Old Testament church had a Harvest Thanksgiving celebration of its own, prescribed in the law. This was the Feast of Tabernacles (Exodus 23:16; Leviticus 23:33-43). It was really much more than a thanksgiving for the harvest. It was to celebrate the way that the Lord had provided for them in the wilderness wanderings in Sinai and how, during that time, they had lived in 'booths' –

temporary shelters made of branches and leaves. Every year, from 15-21 Tishri (a month straddling our September and October), the Israelites were to bring branches, construct booths and live in them, while worshipping and presenting offerings at the temple. This looked back in gratitude for past deliverance and provision but it also looked forward to the future and sought God's blessing for the year to come. It was, for God's people, the 'turn of the year' – their New Year was the first of Tishri and the Day of Atonement was on the tenth of that month. The year had ripened and a new year stretched before them. God had blessed in the past year. He had crowned the year with his goodness (Psalm 65:11). So they turned to prayer for his blessing in the year to come – a prayer they expressed in their praise from Psalm 118:25-28:

> O Lord, save us;
> > O Lord grant us success;
> Blessed is he who comes in the name of the Lord.
> > From the house of the Lord we bless you.
> The Lord is God,
> > and he has made his light shine upon us.
> With boughs in hand, join in the festal procession
> > up to the horns of the altar.
> You are my God and I will give you thanks;
> > You are my God, I will exalt you.

This was the true covenant life of Israel coming into its own – the love of God filling the praise of a people enjoying the fulness of God's richest blessings.

Consider, then, the impact of the vision of the basket of ripe fruit. Did it symbolize fruitfulness and look forward to future blessing, as would have been the case in connection with the Feast of Tabernacles? The answer is a devastating 'No!' **'Then the Lord said to me, "The time is ripe for my people Israel; I will spare them no longer!"'** (8:2) The fruit is picked. There can be no further growth or development. Israel has looked healthy and prosperous but it has been an Indian summer and the end has come. Her wickedness has ripened and the cup of iniquity is full. She is ripe – but for judgement! We all know what happens to overripe fruit. It gets soft and flabby. Fungus begins to erupt on the skin and in a very short time it is ready for the dustbin!

A further declaration underlines the resolve of the Lord to have done with this perverse generation: **'In that day, the songs in the temple will turn to wailing. Many, many bodies – flung everywhere! Silence!'** (8:3) The silence itself is awesome – the irrefutable evidence that God is as good as his word. In the presence of the judgement of God, every mouth will be stopped, for it demonstrates the fact that all men are accountable to God for what they do with his law (Romans 3:19).

Sunset at noon (8:4-10)

The accounting now takes place. The prophet recounts, first of all, what activities they have enjoyed (8:4-6) and then he shows how it will all be turned to ashes and end in utter bitterness and misery (8:7-10).

1. **'Hear this, you who trample the needy and do away with the poor of the land . . .'** (6:4-6). It was a 'devil take the hindmost' society. The national pastime was exploiting the weaker members of the community. The Bible does not teach that the 'needy' were necessarily any better, only that it is gross injustice to oppress anyone. 'Need' is not a virtue, but it provides an opportunity and an obligation for others to do that person some good. Poverty observed ought to issue in poverty relieved! In Israel the exact opposite was the case. Vultures always choose their victims from the disadvantaged of the flock! Israel was less a society and more a food chain, as mutual help and interdependence dissolved in predatory selfishness.

Amos now gives some examples of what occupied their minds (8:5,6).

They just cannot wait for the sabbath to be over, so that they can get on with making money. This recalls an incident I witnessed in Istanbul, Turkey some years ago. After a service in the New Mosque had just concluded, some men ran out ahead of the others, set up portable tables in front of the exits and started selling lottery tickets in their inimitably enthusiastic Levantine fashion! **'When will the New Moon be over . . . and the Sabbath be ended?'** (8:5) is the perennial cry of the hypocrite, whose heart is not in what he is doing. It is interesting that the Israelites at least waited until the sabbath was over! The same cannot be said of many modern Christians with respect to the Lord's Day! Jesus said, 'Unless your righteousness surpasses that of the Pharisees and the teachers of the law, you will certainly not enter the kingdom of heaven' (Matthew 5:20). Our Lord's point is that outward conformity is not enough; there must be a heart-devotion to the scriptural pattern of good behaviour and personal holiness. The Israelites were too busy calculating their profits to be serious about the service of God's house. Outwardly they kept the sabbath, but inwardly they were planning their next swindles. Their minds were on **'skimping the measure, boosting the price and cheating with dishonest scales, buying the poor with silver and the needy for a pair of sandals, selling even the sweepings with the wheat'** (8:6). Jesus, in urging the disciples to sell their possessions and give to the poor that they might have 'treasure in heaven', established the principle that 'Where your treasure is, there your heart will be also' (Luke 12:34). We know where Israel's treasure was, but where is yours?

2. **'I will turn your religious feasts into mourning and all your singing into weeping.'** The injustice of wicked men will be overthrown by the justice of God (8:7-10). 'The unforgiving cannot be forgiven, the unmerciful cannot receive mercy.'[1]

'The Lord has sworn by the Pride of Jacob: "I will never forget anything they have done"' (8:7). The humble believer, always aware of the sinfulness of bad deeds in the eyes of a holy God, asks his heavenly Father to remember his mercy and love and to forget his rebellious ways. That was why teenager Margaret Wilson, tied to a stake in the rising tide of the Solway Firth for the sake of Christ on 11 May 1685, sang the verses of Psalm 25 in the metrical version still used in the praise of Scotland today:

---

[1] J.A. Motyer, *The Day of the Lion*, p. 183.

Thy tender mercies, Lord,
  I pray thee to remember,
And loving-kindnesses; for they
  have been of old forever.

My sins and faults of youth
  do thou, O Lord, forget:
After thy mercy think on me,
  and for thy goodness great   (Psalm 25:6,7).

Forgiveness *is* forgetting (Jeremiah 31:34). But those who stick to their wickedness and refuse to repent and turn to the Lord experience no such gracious forgetting. *Everything* is remembered. Nothing is over-looked. Justice is served. As proud as Israel has been, so the Lord will not forget what they have done.

'Will not the land tremble for this . . .?' (8:8) There will be earthquakes when the reckoning comes.**'I will make the sun go down at noon . . .'** (8:9). There was an eclipse of the sun on 15 June 763 B.C. These events were not as well understood as they are today. An eclipse was invariably taken as a portent of terrible things. This, God appears to have used – a generation before the exile of Israel – to underscore the prophetic witness. The point is that just as these events in nature will surely come about, so the justice of God will overtake their evil deeds. For the joys of their religious feasts, there will be mourning; weeping for singing; sackcloth for luxury and **'the end of it like a bitter day'** (8:10). And this is the way it will be at the end of the present age. Jesus says to those for whom injustice to others is a way of life, '"I tell you the truth, whatever you did not do for one of the least of these, you did not do for me." Then they will go away to eternal punishment, but the rightous to eternal life' (Matthew 25:45,46).

Spiritual famine (8:11-14)

The light of the sun might be eclipsed for a day, but the light of God's Word will be taken away permanently! There will be **'a famine of hearing the words of the Lord'** (8:11). This seems a very strange penalty for a people that had no time for prophets and their ilk. Now they get their heart's desire! Amos will no longer bother the priest of Bethel. Just think how the atheist-humanists and the 'progressive' clergy of the mainline churches in our country would rejoice were it to be made known that all conservative-evangelical elements were to disappear! No one would be there to protest when men who rejected the resurrection of Christ were made bishops of the Church of England! Earnest young men, who believe the Bible ought to be obeyed and preach the necessity of the new birth and personal faith in the historical Jesus, would no longer disturb congregations raised on politics, sociology and choir concerts! The Bible Societies would cease to flood us with 'that book' we never read anyway! And these 'fundamentalists' and their like would not be there to remind us that the Bible has something to say about almost everything in daily life! Our young people would stop coming home with 'testimonies' about how they have become Christians! 'What a relief to be done with that!' you might expect them to say. Is this not the world they are working towards?

Why, then, is 'a famine of hearing the words of the Lord' going to be such a terrible curse to people who have, in any case, steadfastly rejected these words? The answer is that human societies owe much more than they realize to the presence in their midst of the Word of God and those that believe and preach the Saviour revealed in that Word. For example, when the Lord purposed to destroy Sodom for its unparalleled depravity, Abraham pleaded with him to have mercy on them. Abraham presented an argument: 'Will you sweep away the righteous with the wicked?' (Genesis 18:23.) His premise was that it would be unfair to treat the righteous in the same way as the wicked. So the Lord said that for the sake of fifty good people he would spare Sodom. And Abraham argued him down to ten before the conversation was over! (Genesis 18:32.) But Sodom was destroyed. Why? Because there was no one righteous in it. Lot's family, you recall, were led out by the angels from the Lord. When God said to an earlier generation, 'My Spirit will not contend with man for ever' (Genesis 6:3), he was preparing for the flood, which would destroy all but Noah's family. This applies to the church as much as to the societies of men in general. When the Lord says to the church at Ephesus (Revelation 2:1-7), 'If you do not repent, I will come to you and remove your lampstand from its place,' he means that he will remove his presence, his light, the gospel itself. That 'church', in other words, will be no part of *the* church which is the body of Christ and the preacher of his Word in the world! That is why the Ephesian church closed its doors.

The strange thing is that when the Word of God becomes unavailable, the lack of it is felt by the people from whom it has been removed. In everyday experience, we know that when something is in short supply, the demand for it pushes up the price. Scarcity increases demand. It is not the simple economics of supply and demand, however, that creates this heightened interest in the Word. It is the *withdrawal of blessing* – even the blessings that accrue to the wicked through the presence of God's true people among them. Peter Craigie points out that fundamental to the life of Israel was the teaching of Deuteronomy 8:3 that 'Man does not live on bread alone but on every word that comes from the mouth of the Lord.' Craigie comments: 'Ultimately it was God's word that made life possible; by that word the creation of the world was established, by that word redemption was secured from Egyptian slavery, and by that word human beings found the meaning of their lives in relationship with God. The coming famine could culminate in the starvation of the spirit, not the body, but when the spirit dies within a person the carcass is of little value.'[2]

It is because of this fundamental truth as it affects the very nature of man – individuals and societies – that the disastrous consequences which Amos details for us in 8:12-14 inevitably develop and consume the nation and its culture. Three leading symptoms of spiritual collapse are mentioned.

1.   Men will search desperately for '**the word of the Lord, but they will not find it**'. Like everything that is taken for granted and then lost, the Word of the Lord will become the

---

[2] P.C. Craigie, *The Twelve Prophets*, Vol. 1 (St Andrews Press, 1984), p. 186.

object of intense concern. This latter-day zeal for the revealed Word is not all that it may seem to be at first blush. They **'stagger'**, as do drunks in Isaiah 24:20, and ' **wander'** from **'sea to sea'** and from **'north to east'**. That is to say, they rush around in a faithless desperation from the Mediterranean to the Dead Sea and from Dan to the Arabah. They do not go *south*, to the one place where the light of God still shone – namely, in Jerusalem, where God had appointed that he be worshipped! They tried everything but the truth, as do so many in our day that seek 'light' in astrology and the cults! This is a leading characteristic of a dying culture.

2. Young people are affected in a particularly distressing way: **'The lovely young women and strong young men will faint because of thirst.'** Their youth, their beauty and their vigour – the strength and freshness that offer hope for the future – will dissolve in confusion and meaninglessness. Their parents failed them, to be sure, but they are not innocent. They were the Israelite equivalent of the 'drug culture' or the 'drop-out scene' and they 'faint' because what seemed to be an escape from the spiritual bankruptcy on every hand turned out to be a pit from which they saw no escape whatsoever!

3. Others turn, more devotedly than ever, to the old neo-pagan perversion of the true worship of God. **'The shame of Samaria'** and the gods of Dan and Beersheba represent the rump of superstition and syncretism left over, after the substance of God's revealed truth had been chipped away by generation upon generation of alleged theological enlightenment. **'They will fall, never to rise again.'**

There is something else here that is relevant to all these 'seekers' and their 'solutions'. It is the underlying implication that they would still reject the Word of God, were it to be preached to them afresh. The prophet, you see, is giving us an insight into what the Bible calls 'the reprobate mind' (Romans 1:28; 2 Timothy 3:8, AV). It is that state in which a man will seek for 'truth' anywhere, excepting its one and only true source, the Word of God. There is no worse condition for a man to be in.

When we seek to apply these truths to our present situation, we must take great care not to be simplistic and say, for example, 'Our country is just like Israel and our situation is

just as hopeless.' It is true that there is a famine of God's Word
in our country, even in our churches! It is true that the
symptoms of a dying culture are with us and appear to be
worsening, almost by the hour. There is, however, a
fundamental difference between our situation and that of
ancient Israel. That difference is Jesus Christ. We live in a
different phase of the history of redemption because of Jesus
Christ. And this makes all the difference in the world, when we
apply the lessons of the death of Israel. Israel stands as a
monument to God's commitment to his absolute justice and
righteousness. As such, it is a warning to every man and
woman. But God was still faithful to his eternal purpose to save
a people out of this wicked world. His eternal love sent his only
Son, Jesus Christ, to be the mediator of a 'better covenant'
(Hebrews 8:6). Jesus came and died on the cross, bearing the
penalty for sinners in their place. What this means is that, in
terms of the redemptive-historical unfolding of God's purpose
of salvation for humanity, we stand between the first and
second comings of Christ – between the cross and the consummation of all things. This period is called, in Scripture, the
'present age' and 'the last days'. In this New Testament age,
Christ can be preached in fulness, as the risen Saviour. The
Holy Spirit is with the church, as he has been since Pentecost
(Acts 2:1-4). The promises of God's fully revealed covenant of
grace, in Christ, are fresh and powerful, as ever they have been.
The message of Amos was an epitaph for Israel, but as applied
to the New Testament era – our time, these 'last days' – it is a
challenge that calls men and women to Christ. It is a challenge
to Christians to claim the power of the Holy Spirit, that the
knowledge of Christ, as a personal Saviour and Lord, might
extend from sea to sea and to the uttermost parts of the earth,
according to the promise of the Word of God.

We began this study with the Feast of Tabernacles. Jesus
observed that feast in his life upon earth. By his day, a practice
had been established of the priests taking a flagon of water
from the pool of Siloam and pouring it out beside the altar of
burnt-offering in the temple. They associated a verse from the
Scriptures with this ceremony, the words of Isaiah 12:3: 'With
joy you will draw water from the wells of salvation.' This they

associated with the Spirit of God. On the last day of the feast, when this ceremony had been performed, Jesus stood up and said in a loud voice, 'If a man is thirsty, let him come to me and drink. Whoever believes in me, as the Scripture has said, streams of living water will flow from within him' (John 7:37,38). 'By this,' adds the apostle John, 'he meant the Spirit, whom those who believed in him were later to receive. Up to that time the Spirit had not been given, since Jesus had not yet been glorified' (John 7:39). Do you see the connection? Having lived among us, having died on the cross in the place of sinners and having risen and ascended to his kingly reign in the glory of heaven, he has sent the Holy Spirit upon the church (John 14:26; 20:22; Acts 2:1-13). Every believer is a well of that living water, the Holy Spirit within the changed heart and life of every Christian. This is the opposite of a famine of the Word. This is, at one and the same time, our privilege and our challenge as we bring the love of Christ to the people among whom we are set as his ambassadors.

Questions for study and discussion

1. Relate the vision of the basket of ripe fruit to the Feast of Tabernacles. (Leviticus 23:33-43; Psalm 118:25-28.) What aspect of the ripeness of fruit is used to illustrate Israel's position?

2. What kind of a society was that of Israel? (Amos 8:4-6.) What preoccupied them on the sabbath? What light does this shed on your attitudes to the things of God? (Luke 12:35; Matthew 5:20; John 4:24.)

3. Discuss the justice of God in relation to Amos 8:8-10. Read Psalm 73 and Matthew 6:2,5,16 and discuss the 'reward' of the wicked (Compare Romans 6:21-23).

4. What is a famine of the Word of God? Why is God's removal of his Word so devastating? (Genesis 6:3; 18:32; 19:24,25; Revelation 2:1-7; Deuteronomy 8:3.)

5. What is the proper response of the church to the need of our country?

12.
The final verdict

Please read Amos 9:1-10

The fifth and final vision is now revealed to the prophet – and final it is, for it heralds the end of the kingdom of Israel in a manner which allows no possibility of recall. Significantly, Amos uses a different name for God on this occasion. Hitherto, he has used the covenant name, Yahweh, rendered as the capitalized LORD in our English Bibles. Here, he uses 'Adonai' – rendered 'Lord' and meaning 'the one who rules over all' – clearly indicating, as we shall see, a change of relationship between God and Israel. He rejects them as *covenant* people.

The Lord is standing by **'the altar'.** From there, he proclaims his judgement upon **'the sinful kingdom'** (9:8). We are not told whether the altar in view is the false altar of Bethel or the altar in the temple at Jerusalem. The commentators are divided on the question and are able to marshal very respectable reasons for being quite settled in their opinions. It is, perhaps, better left an open question. What Amos sees is a vision, not a video of an actual historical event. Where the altar is is probably irrelevant. The point is that God will destroy the perverted worship of Israel. The vision is not a prediction of an actual appearance of God beside any altar anywhere; it is a prophetic pictorialization of the destruction of *all* the false altars of Israel *and*, indeed, all false worship everywhere in time to come. The central thread throughout the vision is the judgement of God upon covenant-breakers. The immediate object of this divine visitation is Israel (Samaria). The ultimate object is surely the destruction of the temple in Jerusalem and the end of the Old Testament era. There will, of course, be a general judgement at the end of the present age, when the Lord Jesus Christ returns and the whole of history and the plan of redemption is consummated. This would appear to be beyond the immediate scope of this passage, but the holiness of God and the absolute certainty of his just judgement must be a proper avenue of application to all who hear the message of God's Word today.

There are two principal elements to the prophet's final verdict upon Israel. The first is the Lord's rejection of Israel as his covenant people, while the second is the Lord's determination to sift the visible church, thereby removing the chaff of covenant-breaking pretence but saving the kernels of remnant faithfulness. This glimmer of grace is the beginning of a brightening prospect of spiritual revival, as we shall see in the last chapter of these studies.

The seal of disapproval (9:1-6)

Israel's special covenant relationship is fast coming to an end. The four previous visions pointed with increasing intensity to the consequences of rejecting God's will. This final vision portrays the Lord's rejection of Israel as his covenant people, an event which came to melancholy fruition less than half a century after the ministry of the prophet, that is, in 722 B.C., when the kingdom of Israel was destroyed and the people exiled, never to return.

1.   **'Smash the tops of the pillars so that the thresholds shake'** (9:1). The Lord sets his seal of disapproval on Israel by striking the pillars. The place where they thought they could worship God is smashed by his anger at their hypocrisy. Their 'hot line' to heaven was gone! Indeed, it had long been a phantasm in their own minds. It had all been a great mistake! God was really against them!

2.   **'Not one will get away, none will escape'** (9:1-4). The long arm of God's law reaches out to complete the execution of his perfect justice. The severity of the language is most striking. There is no escaping the meaning. This had occasioned considerable controversy. How could a loving God utter such terrible imprecations? Does this not contradict his essential character? Surely not! His justice is the concomitant of his

holiness without being the contradiction of his love. A father, who loves his child and has practised that love in the way he brought up the child, is going to be very deeply wounded and very angry if that child returns only contempt and viciousness. We can understand, in our normal experience, the co-existence of such apparently contradictory feelings. Such 'contradictions' are perhaps better thought of as 'complexities'. These complexities arise because of the fact of sin in the human heart. Sin itself is the ultimate contradiction – the contradiction of God. The true 'difficulty' – if such a word may be used of God – is not that he should decide to annihilate wickedness, but that he should find a way to forgive and save sinners. Christ resolves that contradiction for all who believe, by bearing away their sin and winning a full salvation for them. The love of God is expressed, ultimately, in Christ. Outside of faith in Christ, the anger of God is inevitable. And in the mind of God – the eternal and unchangeable one – the attributes of justice and goodness are in perfect and eternal harmony. Anger in God is itself perfectly good, since it is the expression of revulsion against the contradiction of perfect goodness. When compassion and mercy – themselves rooted in the eternal goodness of God – are contemptuously rejected by men, how can the Lord be anything other than offended to the point of exacting the penalty of disobedience? Therefore, 'none will escape'.

Let us be clear on this point. The love of God itself, as a love for all that is good, requires the satisfaction of justice. Love of good cannot but involve hatred of bad. Forgiveness of sins, as an expression of God's love, also requires satisfaction of justice. Christ, in his sufferings and death, bore the penalty and satisfied the demands of perfect justice. 'He is the atoning sacrifice for our sins . . .' (1 John 2:2). The idea that forgiveness of sin is a kind of heavenly clerical amendment in which God simply erases the entry from the record book is completely foreign to the teaching of the Bible. Sin must be covered by the blood of Christ or its consequences faced in time and eternity. Either way God's justice is served. Either way God's love is inviolate. But whereas he rejoices in sinners being reconciled to him, he takes no pleasure in the death of the wicked.

3. **'The Lord is his name'** (9:5,6). God reinforces the seriousness of these words by reminding Israel that he is the Creator who rules over all the powers of the natural world. His words are not empty rhetoric. He is no 'paper tiger'. He will deliver on his promises: 'The Lord is his name!'

The sifting of the church (9:7-10)

The key expression in these verses is **'the sinful kingdom'** (9:8). This describes the real state of the nation. In their own eyes, however, the Israelites were not that bad at all. It must have been a terrible shock for them to hear that God now regarded them as no different from other nations, the 'lesser breeds without the law', to use Kipling's phrase. **'"Are not you Israelites the same to me as the Cushites?" declares the Lord'** (9:7). The Hebrew text uses the stock phrase, 'sons of Israel', rendered 'Israelites' in the NIV. This expression is used no less than 630 times in the Scriptures! It was connected with their heritage as the people of God. It reminded them that they were special, they were privileged, they were unlike other nations, they were in covenant with the living God! When God uses this language – 'sons of Israel' – in the same breath as a denunciation of them as 'the sinful kingdom', he is exploding their pretensions to being God's 'favourite sons'! Indeed, several expressions are used in this passage in the same way:

1. **'Sons of Israel'** (9:7a). Israel took a great deal of pride and self-satisfaction from her natural lineage. Men like to think that they are *naturally* superior, that is that they are a superior breed. National pride turns easily into out-and-out racism. The Israelites, if anything, went further than racism; they gave themselves the *automatic favour* of God on the basis of their birth and descent. They accepted covenantal privileges, conveniently forgot about the covenantal obligations and took all the glory to themselves. 'Well,' says the Lord, 'you are now hereby declared to be no different from the Cushites, however much you boast about your superior lineage!'

2. **'Did I not bring Israel up from Egypt . . .?'** (9:7b) They comforted themselves with the remembrance of past glories.

Had not God brought *them* from Egypt? Do we not have a glorious past that shows that God is with us? This is a kind of triumphalism not all that different from the self-congratulatory accounts that some modern churches publish to promote their history and present witness. It is right that we praise God for his mighty acts in the past, but it is shameful to use these outpourings of grace as evidence that we have some great merit in ourselves. The Lord reminds Israel that he was just as responsible for the migration of the heathen nations – the Philistines and the Arameans – as he was for that of Israel. Since they had rejected the purpose for which God took them out of Egypt, then the exodus itself had no greater practical significance to them than did the movement of the Philistines from Caphtor (Crete)! There is no perpetual donation of divine favour, just because God happened to do some great deed for their ancestors! They are 'the sinful nation' *now* and their favoured past is more of a reproach to them than any sign of God's approval!

3.   **'Surely the eyes of the Sovereign Lord are upon'** Israel (9:8). They accepted Psalm 34:15 but did not read on into Psalm 34:16.

> The eyes of the Lord are on the righteous
>   and his ears are attentive to their cry;
> The face of the Lord is against those who do evil,
>   to cut off the memory of them from the earth
>   (Psalm 34:15,16).

Men want to feel that God is on their side and that he accepts them 'warts and all'. But God looks at Israel and sees 'the *sinful* kingdom'.

4.   **'Disaster will not overtake or meet us'** (9:10). Whenever a crisis arises in a country, the politicians will immediately play down the problem. Official lies are told in order to allay the fears of the public and prevent panic. Why? Because, from experience, governments know that the mass of the people have great difficulty coping with the truth, especially if it is bad news. 'It cannot happen to us,' was Israel's official lie to herself. That, in effect, is what a person

says to himself, when he rejects the offer of salvation in the gospel of Jesus Christ. Every time he hears the offer of grace, every time he remembers the gospel offer, every time he brushes aside what God has said about his dangerous spiritual condition – every time he is practically saying, 'It will not happen to me. Such disaster will not overtake me. I do not need a Saviour.' Commenting on this perennial addiction to self-deception on the part of unconverted people, John Calvin perceptively observes, 'Security then, which of itself, ever generates a contempt of God, is here mentioned as the principal mark of impiety. And doubtless the vices of men reach a point that is past hope, when they are touched neither by fear nor shame, but expect God's judgements without any concern or anxiety.'[1] They expect *favorable* judgements, of course – hence the lack of anxiety.

The Lord has stripped away the pretensions of Israel. That this is not merely to enlighten that nation as to the reasons for her destruction is evident from two verses embedded in the middle of all the death and destruction. The Lord says, **'I will not totally destroy the house of Jacob, for I will give the command, and I will shake the house of Israel among all the nations as grain is shaken in a sieve, but not a kernel will fall to the ground'** (9:8b,9). There will be a remnant according to the election of grace. God is sifting the Old Testament church: the chaff and the broken kernels will pass through the sieve of refining judgement, while the whole kernels, representing true believers, will be retained. In the long run, the Lord's people will be reconstituted as a revived and faithful church of God. And the proof of this is in all that was revealed in Jesus Christ, in all that the gospel has acccomplished in millions of lives through the ministry of the New Testament church and even, if we may be so bold, in the fact that you, reader of this book, have the gospel preached to you at this moment in your experience. God remembered mercy, in the midst of his wrath. He spoke a word of free grace

---

[1] John Calvin, *Commentaries on the Twelve Minor Prophets*, Vol. XIV (Baker Book House: 1979), p. 402.

to the remnant, even in the midst of the maelstrom of judgement!

The believer is always in the eye of the storm – that place of peace surrounded by fierce buffetings. He is at peace in his heart, whatever may become of his body, because he has the consolation of the Lord's undying love and imperishable promises. 'In this great universe,' wrote Herman Veldkamp, 'there is but one safe place – Golgotha!'[2] When Christ died upon the cross, he drew the sting of death for every believer. He secured redemption for people who were spiritually dead. He won eternal life for a condemned race. And not one of those who have come to him in saving faith will perish, for, as Jesus said, 'I give them eternal life, and they shall never perish; no one can snatch them out of my hand. My Father, who has given them to me, is greater than all; no one can snatch them out of my Father's hand. I and the Father are one' (John 10:28,29).

Surely the Lord is sifting the church today! Surely the meaning of Amos for us is that the church must be always reforming – repenting of the doctrinal and practical departures from, and additions to, the Word of God that have blunted the lively claims of the gospel upon men's hearts and lives; and returning to the Saviour with the resolve, born of the Holy Spirit in the inner man, to be *real* disciples of Jesus Christ. 'So then, just as you received Christ Jesus as Lord, continue to live in him, rooted and built up in him, strengthened in the faith as you were taught, and overflowing with thankfulness' (Colossians 2:6,7).

Questions for study and discussion

1. What does Amos see? Discuss the meaning of the vision. What does it mean when God destroys the place of worship? What does this mean for (a) Israel (2 Kings

---

[2] H. Veldkamp, *The Farmer from Tekoa*, p. 228.

17:7-23); (b) Judah (Jeremiah 24:1-10); (c) The Jews of Jesus' day (Matthew 23:32,38); (d) The present day (1 Thessalonians 4:11-5:11)?

2. Was God justified in dealing with Israel in the manner described in verses 1-4? What were the original terms of the covenant that God had made with Israel? (Deuteronomy 30:15-20. Review Amos 1-8.)

3. Why does Amos stress the teaching that God is the Creator who rules the natural world? (Amos 9:5,6; Job 38:1-10; 40:1-5; Romans 9:20,21.)

4. How does God use the judgement to preserve a remnant? (Amos 9:8b,9; compare John 6:37-44; 10:28,29.)

5. What challenge does Amos set before the modern church? What is the difference between God's programme for Israel in the eighth century B.C. and the church of Jesus Christ in the twentieth /twenty-first centuries A.D.? (Matthew 28:18-20; Philippians 1:6; 2 Corinthians 2:14; Ephesians 5:27; Revelation 21:2.)

13.
The future day of salvation

Please read Amos 9:11-15

The final, climactic vision of Amos depicted both the judgement of God upon his erstwhile people in Israel and, in the sifting of his truly believing people from that decayed portion of the visible church, a bright intimation of hope. Side by side we see the *severance* of covenant privileges, in the case of the apostates within its external administration, and the *establishment* of covenant promise, with reference to those whom the Lord is choosing for himself as his 'treasured possession' (Malachi 3:17). There were those, even in the darkest of days, who 'feared the Lord' and 'talked with each other and the Lord listened and heard. A scroll of remembrance was written in his presence concerning those who feared the Lord and honoured his name. "They will be mine,' says the Lord Almighty . . ."' (Malachi 3:16,17).

The last section of the prophecy takes that note of grace, earlier sounded in Amos 9:8b,9, and develops it into a glorious rhapsody of future restoration and redemption. It is as if the Lord has said to Amos, 'Amos! I have told you to expose, relentlessly, the spiritual darkness of my so-called church in Israel; I have given you the task of telling them of judgements to come; I have, through you, held out a way of escape, in that if they seek me they will live, and I have declared a message of hope for the future for the remnant that remain in my Word. But now, I tell you to show them the latter-day glory of the church of the living God!' For us, who live in the 'last days', this message has its counterpart in the fulness of the New Testament revelation: 'I saw the Holy City, the new Jerusalem, coming down out of heaven from God, prepared as a bride beautifully dressed for her husband. And I heard a loud voice from the throne saying, "Now the dwelling of God is with men, and he will live with them. They will be his people, and God himself will be with them and be their God . . ."' (Revelation 21:2,3).

The prospect in Amos ultimately looks ahead to this great promise of the eternal glory of the church. But to the remnant, struggling to maintain a faithful testimony in dying Israel, the more immediate focus of the promise – the restoration of 'David's fallen tent' – must have seemed as distant as eternity itself. They could only have understood it to refer to the messsianic age.

This magnificent theme is developed in the simplest way. Firstly, we are told of the restoration of 'David's fallen tent' (9:11,12) and, secondly, we are given an account of the glory of the new covenant era (9:13-15).

David's tent restored (9:11,12)

'God,' as Calvin remarks, 'would punish the sins of the people of Israel in such a way as to remember still his own promise.'[1] There will be a restoration and it will involve both the house of David, the king and the children of Israel, the nation.
1. **'In that day I will restore David's fallen tent . . .'** (9:11). The 'day' in view is that in which the Messiah is revealed. This becomes clear from the meaning and significance of the expression, 'David's fallen tent'.

David's 'tent', or 'booth', has a double reference. It recalls the 'booths' in which Israel lived during their wilderness wanderings, which, you will remember from an earlier study, were commemorated in the Feast of Tabernacles.[2] This signified God's gracious provision for Israel throughout her history. It also recalls by way of a contrast, the phrase 'house of

---

[1] J. Calvin, *Commentaries on the Twelve Minor Prophets*, Vol. XIV, p.403.

[2] See the discussion in Chapter 11, pp.110-112.

David', a reference to the dynasty of Davidic kings.[3] Whereas a 'tent' (Hebrew, *sūkâ*) is a temporary shelter, a 'house' (Hebrew, *bayît*) is a permanent building. It is a measure of how far the Davidic monarchy has sunk that it is now called a fallen tent! The theocratic monarchy, as such, still lingered on in Judah. It would fall in the sixth century B.C. How and when would it be restored?

The Lord himself will revive the house of David. **'I will restore . . . I will repair its broken places, restore its ruins and build it as it used to be . . .'** There will be a new king (Hosea 1:11; Ezekiel 37:22) who, according to promise will 'sit on your throne [i.e. David's] for ever and ever' (Psalm 132:12). And this is none other than the Lord Jesus Christ, the 'Lord' to whom 'the Lord' will say, 'Sit at my right hand until I make your enemies a footstool for your feet' (Psalm 110:1).

His kingdom will extend to the four corners of the earth (Psalm 22:27-31; 45:4-6; 72:8-11,17-19; 89:27-29,34-37) and its glory will be that it is the very temple of the Holy Spirit, the church, the body of Christ (1 Corinthians 3:16; Ephesians 2:19-22; 1 Peter 2:4-6). In the twilight of theocratic Israel, the fallen tent of David will be Joseph and Mary. The new King will be born in the stench and dirt of a stable in Bethlehem. The true royal family of Israel and Judah was not that of Herod, the Idumean, but that of the Nazareth carpenter and his expectant wife!

2. The restored Davidic kingdom will **'possess the remnant of Edom and all the nations that bear my name . . .'** (9:12). In other words, when Christ is revealed, the separation between Israel and the nations will be at an end. People from all nations will make up the covenant people of God and share privileges hitherto restricted to Israel. The promise is universal in that Christ's rule in the hearts of

---

[3]J.A. Motyer (*The Day of the Lion,* pp. 202-203) proposes an intriguing if rather speculative, explanation of the idea of the 'booth' of David; tying it in with the Melchizedek priesthood and thus linking its restoration to Christ as the great High Priest after the order of Melchizedek. There is a helpful footnote (3) on some critical questions relative to the integrity of the text.

men will extend to every nation and every tongue on earth.

'Edom' is mentioned because she was the most intransigent enemy of Israel (Amos 1:11,12; cf. Numbers 20:14-21; Judges 11:17; 2 Samuel 8:14; 1 Kings 11:14-17). Her overthrow symbolizes the overthrow of the most vigorous opposition. The 'remnant of Edom' signifies that even from this most wicked of nations there shall be people saved by the Lord Jesus Christ.

The nations *'that bear my name'* are a reference to the inroads that the gospel will make into all the nations of the world. The day will come when the kingdoms of this world will become the kingdom of our Lord and of his Christ (Revelation 11:15). In the Old Testament, a conquered city is named for its conqueror (2 Samuel 12:28). Thus the nations are *'possessed'* or conquered by Christ. 'This mystery,' writes Paul, 'is that through the gospel the Gentiles are heirs together with Israel, members together of one body, and sharers together in the promise in Christ Jesus' (Ephesians 3:6; cf. Acts 15:13-18). Elsewhere, the apostle assures Christians: 'You are all sons of God through faith in Christ Jesus, for all of you who were baptized into Christ have been clothed with Christ. There is neither Jew nor Greek, slave nor free, male nor female, for you are all one in Christ Jesus. If you belong to Christ, then you are Abraham's seed, and heirs according to the promise' (Galatians 3:26-29).

The new Davidic kingdom, in Jesus Christ the son of David, reverses for an elect remnant the terrible situation which was outlined in the first two chapters of Amos's prophecy. The new kingdom is 'not of this world' (John 18:36). The weapons of its warfare are spiritual and they have 'divine power to demolish strongholds' (2 Corinthians 10:3-6). The gospel of salvation through the blood of Christ, shed in atonement for the sins of men and women, is for all nations. In Christ, the lost sheep of Israel are gathered in and David's royal throne is re-established. Jesus Christ is King and Head of the church, his body, and rules over all for the benefit of his people. The old Israel is revived as the true Israel of God in Christ by his victorious sufferings, death and resurrection. History itself is under his rule from the right hand of the Majesty in heaven (Ephesians 1:20-23; Hebrews 1:3; 8:1).

The glory of the church (9:13-15)

The glory of the era of the new covenant is now described.
What is in view is the New Testament age, culminating in the
future glory of the new heavens and the new earth which will be
ushered in by the return of the Lord Jesus Christ. The picture
of the church that is now presented refers to both the present
time and the future eternal state. The promises of God for the
church are both 'now' and 'not yet'. Between the two advents
of Christ, the church labours as his ambassador, sowing the
seed of the gospel, reaping the harvest of those who believe in
the Lord Jesus Christ and reclaiming a lost world for the
lordship of the Saviour. This advance takes place against the
opposition of the false faiths that possessed virtually every
square inch of the globe at the time of Christ's crucifixion. The
true church in the whole world would not have filled many
modern church halls! (Acts 1:15.) From such a tiny beginning,
the gospel message spread from province to province
throughout the Roman Empire and from there to the
continents of the world. This has been, as the Bible says, a
'warfare' (2 Corinthians 10:4; Revelation 17:14). The battle is
spiritual, but no less real for that. The tide of that battle ebbs
and flows. There are times of spiritual revival and reformation
and periods of relative decline, all varying with time and place.
But the spread of the gospel continues on towards the goal,
which will be consummated with the return of Christ and the
end of these 'last days'. Then the fulness of God's promises –
that which has been in the 'not yet' category, while awaiting
the Day of the Lord – will be revealed in the eternal fruition of
his purposes for his people.

It is these promises – those which belong to the church 'now'
and will be experienced in all their fulness in heavenly glory
that is 'not yet' – that God now declares through the prophet
Amos.

1. **'The days are coming ... when the reaper will be
overtaken by the ploughman and the planter by the one
treading grapes'** (9:13). This recalls the promise of Leviticus
26:3-5: 'If you follow my decrees and are careful to obey my
commands, I will send you rain in its season, and the ground

will yield its crops and the trees of the field their fruit. Your threshing will continue until grape harvest and the grape harvest will continue until planting, and you will eat all the food you want and live in safety in your land.'

Here is the true answer to the miseries of famine in this world – claim God's promises in obedience and in diligence. The point is that in Christ the effects of the curse (Genesis 3:17,18) are rolled back. God blesses the whole of man's life when that life is renewed by Jesus Christ, through living faith in him. These promises are not primarily, far less exclusively, about the agricultural effects of the Fall. The primary focus is upon the abundant life – spiritual and temporal – of the kingdom of God. This applies to the church in the present age and to the church in the glory of the eternal heavenly kingdom. It is the church preaching Christ to a world in deep trouble. It is the Lord adding to the church daily those who are being saved (Acts 2:47). It is the establishment of Christian families and covenant life in the home (Deuteronomy 6:6-9; Ephesians 6:1-4). It is God-honouring industrial relations (Ephesians 6:5-9; 1 Peter 2:13-25). It is government upholding national righteousness (Proverbs 20:26; Romans 13:1-7). It is Jesus Christ converting sinners to himself and leavening his world with the light of the gospel – put into practice through a lively obedience to the whole Word of God. This will continue till the end of our age and issue in the perfect glory of the church in heaven.

2. **'I will bring back my exiled people Israel . . .'** (9:14). The judgement of Amos 5:11 will be reversed. The church will be restored to its privileges in even greater measure in the New Testament era. 'Cities and countries wasted by sin and unbelief, supersitition and vice, are rebuilt by the preaching of God's Gospel, as the history of the Church during the past twenty centuries proves.'[4] The Lord's people will enjoy the fruits of the Holy Spirit (Isaiah 55:1-7; Jeremiah 31:31-34; Galatians 5:22-25; Revelation 22:1-5).

3. **'I will plant Israel in their own land, never again to be**

---

[4] T. Laetsch *The Minor Prophets* (Concordia, 1956), p.192.

uprooted from the land I have given them' (9:15). This is
the language of eternal security. The church of Jesus Christ
will never be deprived of its inheritance. Calvin has a lovely
thought on this: 'But now God declares that his grace would
outweigh the sins of the people; as though he said, "However
unworthy the people are who dwell in this land, my gift will yet
be effectual: for I will not regard what they deserve at my
hands, but as I have given them this land, they shall obtain
it."'[5] The fulfilment is not in some literal and perpetual re-
establishment of an Israelitish state, but is, in keeping with the
imagery of the passage, in the 'kingdom of God . . . propagated
among all nations, from the rising to the setting of the sun'.[6]
The blessing of God is assured for every believer, both now and
for eternity. Jesus said, 'I give them eternal life, and they shall
never perish' (John 10:27). 'For those God foreknew he also
predestined to be conformed to the likeness of his Son, that he
might be the first-born among many brothers. And those he
predestined, he also called; those he called, he also justified;
those he justified, he also glorified' (Romans 8:29,30). And this
is why the apostle can say, 'And we know that in all things God
works for the good of those who love him, who have been called
according to his purpose' (Romans 8:28). From being chosen
in Christ from before the creation of the world (Ephesians 1:3),
through being sustained as those in whom the Holy Spirit is
completing a good work' (Ephesians 1:13; Philippians 1:6) and
coming, at length, to their inheritance in glory in the presence
of their Father God, the Lord's people truly possess the 'land'
that God has given to them in his great love and mercy. It is the
church of Jesus Christ – the holy nation (1 Peter 2:9) – that is
the solid ground amid the shifting sands of human history and
destiny. It is the triumph of the church – '*more* than conquerors'
through Christ who loved sinful men and women enough to die
for them (Romans 8:37) – that she will outlast all other forces
and prevail against the very gates of hell (Matthew 16:18) to be
the permanent possession of the Lord!

---

[5] J. Calvin, *Commentaries on the Twelve Minor Prophets*, Vol. XIV, p.412.
[6] J. Calvin, *Commentaries on the Twelve Minor Prophets*, Vol. XIV, p.413.

The Lord your God (9:15)

The prophecy ends with the words, **'says the Lord your God'**. Israel's rejection as a covenant people was signalled at the beginning of the ninth chapter by the identification of God, as he stood by the altar (9:1), as 'Adonai' – the Almighty, ruler of heaven and earth. With the promise to the remnant of believers that Israel will be revived and triumph completely through the rule of the Messiah, he identifies himself again as 'Yahweh' – the Father God of the covenant of grace with his people. God has committed himself anew and he will surely accomplish his purpose of grace in his appointed time (Numbers 23:19).

As this mighty and inexorable movement of the purpose of God advances to that day when sin and death will be completely vanquished, the practical experience of the church can be less than triumphant. There are days 'of small things' (Zechariah 4:10) and times of great revival when the Holy Spirit is poured out in great power (Isaiah 45:8). Our own country has seen very notable spiritual revivals in each century since the Reformation, excepting the twentieth century – so far. There have been dark interludes of spiritual and moral decay in both church and (therefore) nation. Over a century of radical criticism of the Bible and its authority – what we often call 'theological liberalism' – has left many churches without a Bible that is regarded as God's inerrant Word, without a corpus of doctrine that expresses systematically the exclusive claims of that Word, without any meaningful concept, or practice, of discipleship and personal devotion to Jesus Christ and without any moral absolutes to guide the lives of men and women and society as a whole. Through this long night of spiritual and moral declension, so disturbingly similar to Amos's Israel, the prayer of faithful believers has been for a Holy Spirit-wrought revival of the order of the Reformation to sweep through the land. This highlights the fact that the promise of the triumph of the church is one that must be repeatedly claimed by believers in succeeding generations until the Lord Jesus returns on that day. The church may look at times to be more like 'David's fallen tent' than the glorious body of Christ! And it is a sad fact that much of what calls itself

'the church' has gone over to the enemy. It is the 'antichrists'
who have fashioned so much of modern theology and blasted
the spiritual vitality of so many churches (1 John 2:18-27).
Jesus was perfectly clear on this point, needless to say. In the
parable of the persistent widow, which teaches both the
necessity of persistent prayer in the face of a hostile and unjust
world and the certainty of God's vindication of his elect, our
Lord asks, 'However, when the Son of Man comes, will he find
faith in the earth?' (Luke 18:8.) The triumph of the gospel is
gained by the most earnest contending for the faith that was
once for all entrusted to the saints (Jude 3). The gates of hell
can never prevail against the church (Matthew 16:18). The
true church *is* powerful to 'demolish strongholds' (2
Corinthians 10:4). The triumph of the gospel is seen in the true
church, 'the church of the first-born, whose names are written
in heaven' (Hebrews 12:23), as she actually *lives* the new life
that she has in Christ.

When there is an ebbing of faithfulness in the life of the
individual believer, he says with the psalmist,

> 'Restore to me the joy of your salvation
>   and grant me a willing spirit, to sustain me'.
> >   (Psalm 51:12).

And with the prophet Habakkuk he prays,

> 'Lord, I have heard of your fame;
>   I stand in awe of your deeds, O Lord.
> Renew them in our day,
>   in our time make them known;
>   in wrath remember mercy'
> >   (Habakkuk 3:2).

Then the Christian rejoices with Isaiah in the promises of God:

> 'Build up, build up, prepare the road!
>   Remove the obstacles out of the way of my people.'
> For this is what the high and lofty One says—
>   he who lives for ever, whose name is holy:

'I live in a high and holy place,
  but also with him who is contrite and lowly in spirit,
to revive the spirit of the lowly
  and to revive the heart of the contrite'
                              (Isaiah 57:14,15).

Therefore with the apostle John we say, 'Amen, Come, Lord Jesus' (Revelation 21:20).

'The grace of the Lord Jesus be with God's people. Amen'
                              (Revelation 21:21).

Questions for study and discussion

1. What is David's tent and in what respects will it be restored? (See Psalm 132:12; 110:1; 72:8-11,17-19; 1 Peter 2:4-6.)
2. How does the church *conquer* the nations? (2 Corinthians 10:3-6; Ephesians 1:20-23; Galatians 3:26-29.)
3. Discuss the present experience of the New Testament church in relation to the promises given about its glory in Amos 9:13-15. What is the distinction between the 'now' of God's promises and the 'not yet' of these same promises? What should our faithful response involve? (See Matthew 28:19,20; Deuteronomy 6:5-9; Ephesians 6:1-4; 1 Peter 2:13-25; Proverbs 20:26; 1 Timothy 2:2.)
4. Discuss the present need of revival in this country. (Compare Zechariah 4:10 and Isaiah 45:8.) Will the church ever be extinguished? (Matthew 16:18; 2 Corinthians 10:4.)
5. What attitudes and actions are consistent with a desire for revival and, indeed, the outpouring of God's blessing in revival? (Psalm 51:12; Isaiah 57:14,15.)
6. Why will the church triumph? (1 Corinthians 15:20,57; Numbers 23:19; Revelation 22:6.)

Other volumes
in the
Welwyn Commentary Series

The Gospel as it Really is
Paul's Epistle to the Romans simply explained

Stuart Olyott

Perhaps no other book has had as profound an influence on the history of the Christian church as Paul's Epistle to the Romans. It was the discovery of the real message of Romans by Martin Luther which caused him to break away from the church of Rome and become a leader of the Reformation. Many others, before and since, among them Augustine, John Bunyan and John Wesley, have owed their conversion to the teaching of this epistle.

Luther said of Romans: 'It can never be read or considered too much or too well, and the more it is handled, the more delightful it becomes and the better it tastes.'

In this book the author aims to present a simple introduction to Romans for the ordinary reader. His exposition goes straight to the heart of the passage, avoiding technicalities or obscure textual criticism.

The Mystery of Christ
Meditations on Colossians

Guy Appéré

Written in response to the problems of a small church in Asia Minor during the first century A.D., Paul's letter to the Colossians is still highly relevant in this modern age of dissatisfaction and moral confusion.

The solution it offers in such situations, be they past or present; is not some heroic spiritual effort to rise above ourselves, but the divine person of Jesus Christ, in whom we are made complete by virtue of his work of redemption.

Guy Appéré, pastor of a church in Geneva, takes us through the epistle, drawing out the practical application of its profound message.

Dare to Stand Alone
Read and enjoy the Book of Daniel

Stuart Olyott

Here is a commentary for those who would like to read and enjoy the book of Daniel. The symbolism and apparently mysterious passages in the book have discouraged many from giving it serious study. But Stuart Olyott, in his lively yet thorough style, shows that the prophecy of Daniel is basically an easy book to understand. His aim is to excite the reader to read Daniel for himself.

The book of Daniel is full of practical help - especially for believers who find themselves standing alone in the classroom or at work, or among their family and friends. Daniel tells us how to remain true to God in a hostile environment, and shows us how to live for him when everything is against us. Daniel dared to stand alone. So can we.

A Life Worth Living and a Lord Worth Loving
Ecclesiastes & Song of Solomon

Stuart Olyott

Has life really got any meaning? Our time in this world is comparatively short. The earthly stage remains, but different actors are constantly passing across it. Generations come and go, but nothing is ultimately different.

This is how many people see life, and Solomon identifies with them. But is life really pointless? If not, what is its true meaning?

The message of Ecclesiastes is that life is not worth living unless we live it for God. The Song of Solomon teaches us that living for the Lord means loving him.

As in his other popular commentaries, Stuart Olyott gives a heart-warming and practical explanation of the message of these two Old Testament books. They are books full of meaning and challenge for today.